Contents

1 Introducing geography

The big picture

Welcome to *geog.scot1*, the first book of the *geog.scot12* course.

This course is all about planet Earth, and how and where we live on it. These are the big ideas behind the course:

- Humans like us have been here for a very short time, compared to the Earth. (For about 200 000 years, compared with 4.6 billion!)
- We have spread over most of the Earth, farming it, mining it, building on it, and carving it up into over 200 countries.
- We have changed the Earth as we spread – and spoiled many places.
- Now we are learning that we must look after it properly.
- The Earth still holds many dangers for us, such as floods and earthquakes. We try to protect ourselves from them.

Your goals for this course

By the end of this course, we hope you'll be a good geographer! And that means you will:

- be interested in the world around you.
- understand that many processes, both natural and human, are shaping and changing the Earth.
- know what kinds of questions to ask, to find out about countries and places and people.
- be able to carry out enquiries, to find answers to your questions.
- have the other key skills (such as map reading) that a geographer needs. Your teacher will tell you which ones.
- think geography is just brilliant!

Did you know?
- The Earth has been here about 23 000 times longer than humans.

Did you know?
- Dinosaurs were around for about 165 million years.
- That's over 800 times longer than humans!

Did you know?
Most experts think that:
- humans like us first appeared in East Africa ...
- ... and spread out from there.

Did you know?
- Humans like us have been in Scotland for around 11000 years.

Your chapter starter

Page 4 shows a planet. Which one?

Where in space is it?

What's keeping it there?

Who's on it?

What are they doing?

It's the third one from the sun.

In this unit you will find out about the kinds of things we study in geography – and how being nosy will help!

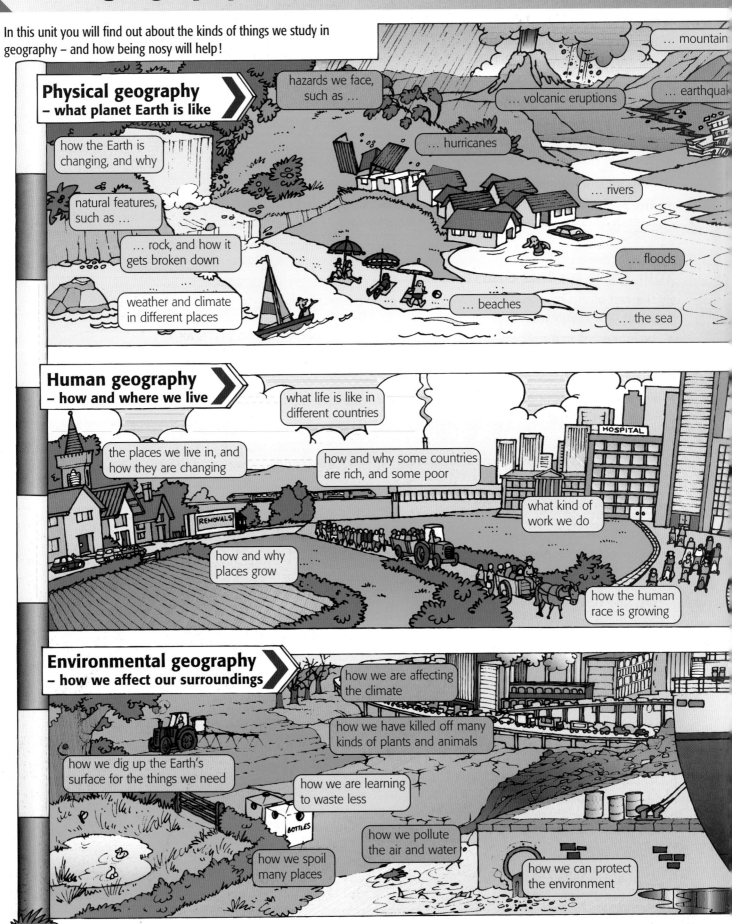

Physical geography
– what planet Earth is like

hazards we face, such as …

… mountain

… volcanic eruptions

… earthquak[e]

… hurricanes

how the Earth is changing, and why

… rivers

natural features, such as …

… rock, and how it gets broken down

… floods

weather and climate in different places

… beaches

… the sea

Human geography
– how and where we live

what life is like in different countries

the places we live in, and how they are changing

how and why some countries are rich, and some poor

HOSPITAL

REMOVALS

what kind of work we do

how and why places grow

how the human race is growing

Environmental geography
– how we affect our surroundings

how we are affecting the climate

how we have killed off many kinds of plants and animals

how we dig up the Earth's surface for the things we need

how we are learning to waste less

BOTTLES

how we pollute the air and water

how we spoil many places

how we can protect the environment

The big big idea

There is one big big idea behind all of geography: everything is always changing.

The Earth's surface is changing. How and where we live is changing. How we affect the Earth is changing.

So, get ready to geog!

The first step to being good at geography is: get nosy!

Use your eyes. Look for clues. Ask questions that start with *Who, What, Where, How, Why, When* …

And enjoy it!

What is it like?

Why is it like this?

Where is this place?

How is it changing?

Who is affected by the changes?

How do they feel about it?

How do *I* feel about it?

Your turn

1 Copy and complete in your own words:
Physical geography is about …
Human geography is about …
Environmental geography is about …

2 Which kind of geography is this topic?
  a how clouds form   b looking for work
  c protecting pandas d where trainers are made
  e caves   f acid rain

3 Photo **A** below shows people on holiday.
  a Why do you think they chose this place?
     List as many reasons as you can.
  b After each reason, write *(P)* if it's about physical geography, *(H)* if human, or *(E)* if environmental.

4 Time to get nosy! Study photo **B** for clues.
  Then answer these questions:
  a What is going on in the photo?
  b How did the place get to be like this?
  c Who do you think is responsible?

5 a Now make up three new questions about photo **B**, and what's going on there. No silly ones!
    (Hint: *Who? What? Where? How? Why? When?*)
  b Ask your partner to try to answer them.

6 Compare the two photos.
  a Can you see any similarities?
  b Do you think there is any connection at all between the two scenes?

A

B

Making and mapping connections

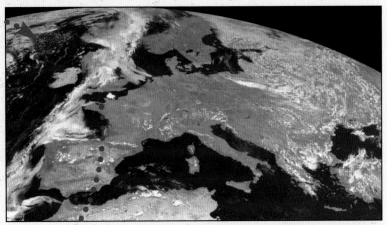

Where is Arthur?

On planet Earth, with over 6.6 billion other humans (that's 6 600 000 000) including you …

… in Europe, with over 807 million other humans (that's 807 000 000) …

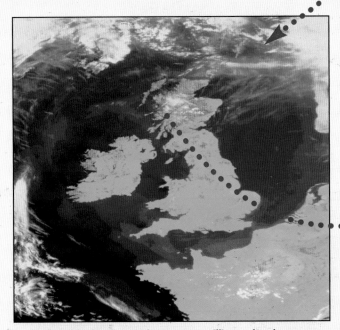

… in the British Isles, with over 64 million other humans …

Ben Nevis

Loch Linnhe

… in Fort William, with over 10 000 other humans …

… in number 31A Kennedy Road, with 4 other humans …

DO NOT ENTER

… and in this room, all alone.

The big picture

This chapter is all about maps, and how to use them. These are the big ideas behind the chapter:

◆ We humans are spread out all over the Earth – but we are still connected to each other in many different ways.

◆ We use maps to show where we live on the Earth, and what places are like.

◆ There are many different kinds of maps.

◆ Using maps is a key skill for a good geographer. (That's you!)

Your goals for this chapter

By the end of this chapter you should be able to answer these questions:

◆ In what ways am I connected to people and places all over the world?

◆ What does the scale on a map or plan tell me?

◆ What are map grid references, and how do I use them to find places?

◆ How can I measure distance on a map?

◆ What are compass points, and how can I use them to give, and follow, directions?

◆ What's the difference between a sketch map and other types of map?

◆ What are OS maps, and what kinds of things are shown on them?

◆ How is the height of the land shown on an OS map? (Two ways!)

◆ What do these terms mean?

    equator   *prime meridian*   *latitude*   *longitude*

◆ How do I tell the latitude and longitude of a place, using a map? How do I find it using an atlas index?

And then ...

When you finish the chapter, come back to this page and see if you have met your goals!

Did you know?

◆ 5000 years ago we thought the Earth was flat – and you could fall off.

Did you know?

◆ The world's oldest known maps were found in Iraq.
◆ They are drawn on clay tablets, over 4500 years old.

Did you know?

◆ Today map makers use photos from satellites and planes, to help them map the world.
◆ 200 years ago, they used the position of the sun and stars.

Your chapter starter

You are flying back to planet Earth to find Arthur.

You have his address – but you don't want to ask for directions.

Would the images on page 8 help you to find him? Give your reasons.

There are special diagrams that would help you much more. Geographers just adore them. They're called ......?

Where have you been?

Making connections

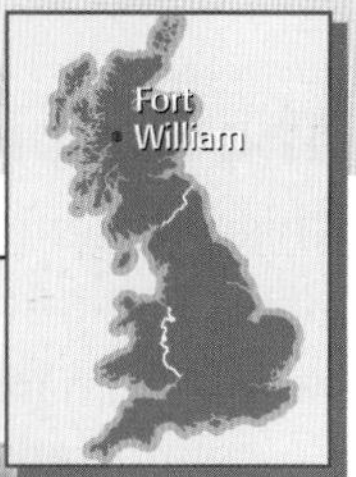

In this unit you'll see how we are connected to people and places all over the world – and how this can be shown using maps.

Arthur connected

Arthur. Alone in his room in Fort William – but connected to people and places everywhere.

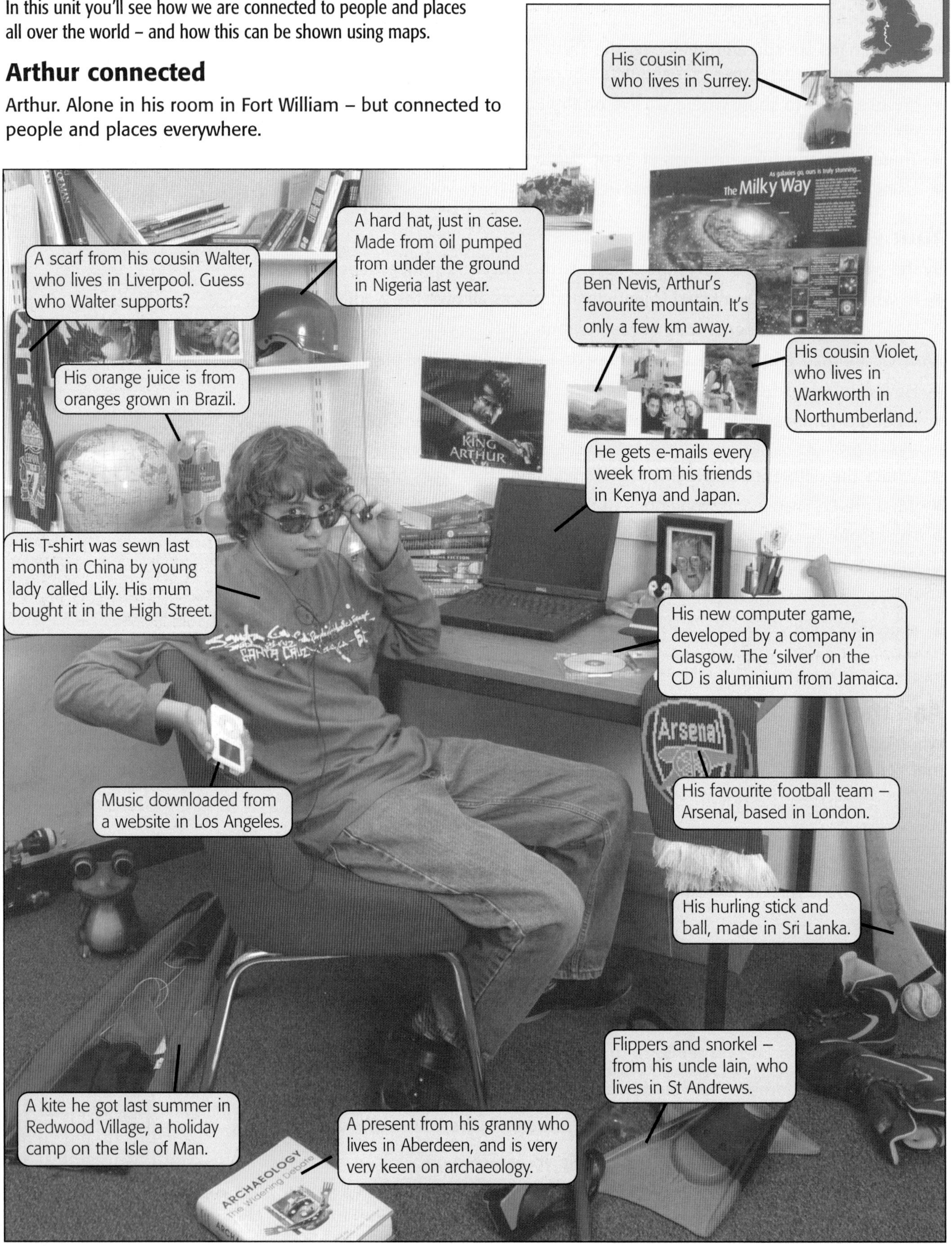

Fort William

His cousin Kim, who lives in Surrey.

A scarf from his cousin Walter, who lives in Liverpool. Guess who Walter supports?

A hard hat, just in case. Made from oil pumped from under the ground in Nigeria last year.

The Milky Way
As galaxies go, ours is truly stunning...

Ben Nevis, Arthur's favourite mountain. It's only a few km away.

His orange juice is from oranges grown in Brazil.

His cousin Violet, who lives in Warkworth in Northumberland.

KING ARTHUR

He gets e-mails every week from his friends in Kenya and Japan.

His T-shirt was sewn last month in China by young lady called Lily. His mum bought it in the High Street.

His new computer game, developed by a company in Glasgow. The 'silver' on the CD is aluminium from Jamaica.

Arsenal

Music downloaded from a website in Los Angeles.

His favourite football team – Arsenal, based in London.

His hurling stick and ball, made in Sri Lanka.

Flippers and snorkel – from his uncle Iain, who lives in St Andrews.

A kite he got last summer in Redwood Village, a holiday camp on the Isle of Man.

A present from his granny who lives in Aberdeen, and is very very keen on archaeology.

ARCHAEOLOGY
The Widening Debate

Mapping connections

Great Britain

The world

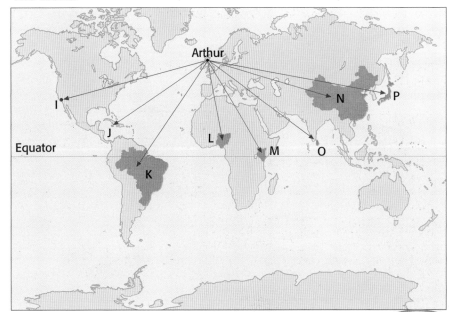

Page 8 showed images of the world, and Europe, and the island where Arthur lives (Great Britain). Above are maps of these places.

With maps it is easier to see where places are, and to show connections between them.

The maps above show Arthur's connections from page 10 – but that is just the start. All day long he is connected to *hundreds* of people and places – through school, TV, the internet, the things he owns, and the food he eats.

It's just the same for you. It's exciting!

Lily in China, who sewed Arthur's top. ▶

Did you know?

◆ By September 2006, over 1.1 billion people were connected via the internet!

Your turn

1 Match each letter on the maps above to a place named on page 10. Start like this: **A** =
  (No peeking at the maps at the back of this book!)
  Then give your answers to a partner to check.

2 Arthur is connected to Jamaica by his new games CD. That's an *international* connection. Pick out:
  a two other international connections for him
  b two local connections
  c two national connections
  (Try the glossary?)

3 You too are connected to hundreds of places.
  a Make a big table like the one started on the right.
  b Leave room for three places, for each connection. Add more types of connection. (Music, TV, clothes?)
  c Now fill in the table, for yourself.

4 Imagine the UK is cut off from the rest of the world. You can't get news, or post, or TV, or phone calls, or food, or other goods, from outside the UK.
  a List all the things you would have to do without.
  b What three things would you miss most?

Places I am connected to

Place	Connection
London	
...	I've been there
...	
...	
...	Friends/relatives live there
...	
...	
...	I eat food that was grown there

Plans and scales

In this unit you will learn what a plan is, and what the scale of the plan tells you.

A photo

This is one corner of Arthur's room. He tidied it a bit for the photo.

A plan

This is a **plan** of Arthur's room – a drawing of what you would see looking down from the ceiling.

A plan is really a map of a small area – for example a room, or a house, or your school.

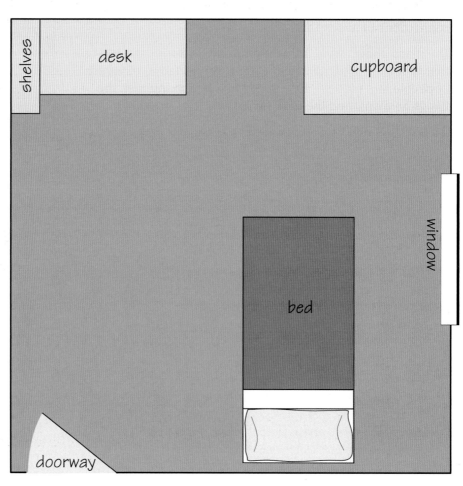

The scale

1 cm on the plan represents 30 cm in the room. That is the **scale** of the plan. You can show it in three ways:

1 In words: **1 cm to 30 cm**

2 As a ratio: **1 : 30**
(say it as *1 to 30*)

3 As a line divided into centimetres:

0   30   60   90   120 cm

The scale is marked on a plan so that people can tell the size in real life.

12

Working out scale

This is the plan of a table in Arthur's kitchen. The table is 8 cm long in the plan. It is 160 cm long in real life.

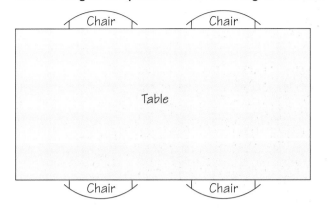

Be careful with units!
Look at this scale.

0   2   4   6   8   10   12 m

Here 1 cm represents 2 metres.
You can write this as **1 : 200**.

The 2 metres has been changed to centimetres. That's because *you must use the same units on each side of the* :

1 : 200 means **1 cm to 200 cm** or **1 cm to 2 m**.

◆ 8 cm on the plan represents 160 cm in real life.

◆ So 1 cm on the plan represents 20 cm in real life.

◆ So you can write the scale as:

1 : 20   or   1 cm to 20 cm   or   0   20   40 cm

Your turn

1 When Arthur sits at his desk, which is to his right?

 a the door   b the window

2 On a plan, one wall of a room is shown like this:

_____

 The scale of the plan is 1 cm to 60 cm.
 How long is the wall in real life?

3 Below are walls from another plan. This time the scale is 1 : 50. How long is each wall in real life?

 a _____

 b _____

4 Using a scale of 1 cm to 20 cm, draw a line to represent:

 a 40 cm   b 80 cm   c 2 metres
 Write the scale beside your lines.

5 If the scale is 1 : 300, what length does each line represent? Give your answer in metres.

 a _____

 b _____

 c _____

6 Draw a line to represent 1 kilometre, using each of these scales in turn:

 1 cm to 1 km   1 cm to 50 m   1 cm to 100 m
 Write the scale beside your line, in any of the three forms you wish.

7 Make a chart like this and fill it in for Arthur's room.

Arthur's room	On the plan	In real life
How wide is it? Measure the wall by the desk.		
How long?		
How long is the bed?		
How wide is the window?		
How wide is the doorway?		

8 Arthur is getting a new chest of drawers for his room:

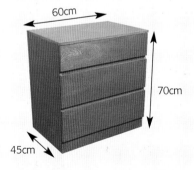

60cm
70cm
45cm

 a To draw a plan of it, which surface will you use?
  the top   the side   the front
 b Draw the plan, to the same scale as Arthur's room.
 c Will the chest of drawers fit through the doorway?
 d Where in the room would you put it?

9 Give three things in the photo of Arthur's room that are not on the plan. Suggest reasons why they're not.

10 How would you set about drawing a plan of *your* room?

13

Maps and grid references

In this unit you will learn how to find places on a map, using grid references.

An aerial photo

This is an **aerial photo** – a photo taken from the air.

It shows part of the River Mole valley in Surrey. In the top right is the village of Mickleham.

Arthur went fishing here when he visited his cousin Kim. (The fish fled.)

Did you know?

◆ *The first ever aerial photo was taken in France, in 1758 – from a balloon!*

A map

This is a **map** of the same place. Compare it with the photo.

Note that the map has:

◆ a title
◆ a frame around it
◆ an arrow to show north
◆ a scale
◆ a key.

A good map should have all of those. This map has **grid lines** too. What do you think they are for?

The River Mole valley near Mickleham

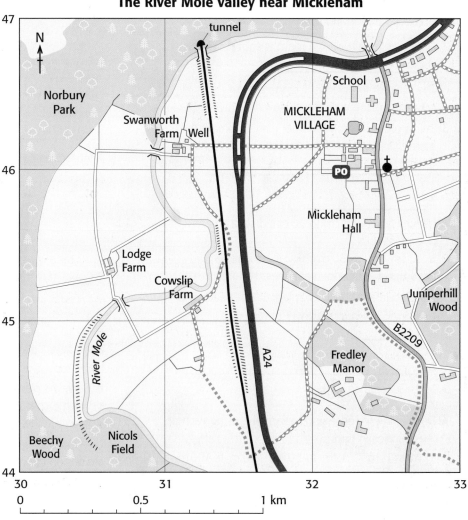

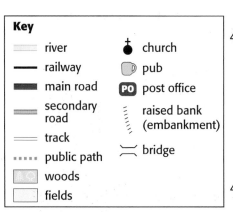

Key

▭ river	✝ church
— railway	⬭ pub
▬ main road	**PO** post office
▭ secondary road	⦚ raised bank (embankment)
═ track	
⋯ public path	⌣ bridge
▣ woods	
▢ fields	

Using grid lines

The grid lines on the map on page 14 are to help you find a place quickly.
To find the school in the square with **grid reference** 3246:

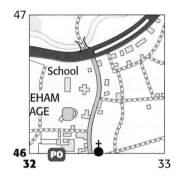

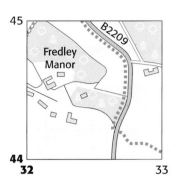

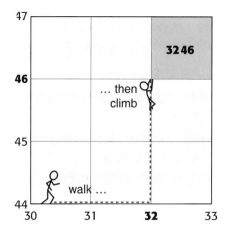

Find the square where lines 32 and 46 meet in the bottom left corner. (It's shown above.) Then look for the school.

In the same way Fredley Manor is in the square with grid reference 3244. Lines 32 and 44 meet in the bottom left corner.

A grid reference gives the number along the bottom first. This shows how to find square 3246. *Walk before you climb!*

These grid references are called **four-figure**. Why?

Six-figure grid references

There is a school *and* a church in square 3246 above.

You can say exactly where each is in the square using a six-figure number. This is what to do:

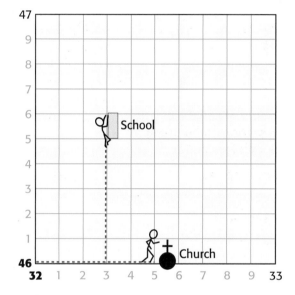

◆ Divide the sides of the square into ten parts, in your mind, as shown on the right.

◆ Count how many parts you must walk through before you reach the building, and how many parts you must climb through.

For the school you go 3 parts along, and 5 parts up.
So its **six-figure grid reference** is 323465.
The one for the church is 325460. Do you agree?

Your turn

1 Look back at the map on page 14. Give a four-figure grid reference for:
   a Mickleham Hall b Cowslip Farm c Nicols Field

2 What is at this grid reference on the map?
   a 312468 b 308448 c 309461

3 Give a six-figure grid reference for:
   a Mickleham Hall
   b the post office
   c the pub

4 There is something at 312463 that you can't see on the photo. What is it?

5 You can't see the river on the photo. How can you tell where it is?

6 Describe what you will see, if you stand at 313453 facing south. (With your back to the north!)

7 How far is it from Lodge Farm to Cowslip Farm, along the track? (Think of a way to measure it using the scale.)

8 This shows a signpost in the area. Where do you think it belongs on the map? See if you can suggest a six-figure grid reference for it.

9 Now compare the map on page 14 with the plan on page 12.
   a In what ways are they alike?
   b In what ways are theydifferent?

How far?

In this unit you will learn how to find the distance between two places on a map.
You will need a strip of paper with a straight edge.

1 As the crow flies

'As the crow flies' means the straight line distance between two places.
To find the straight line distance from A to F, this is what to do:

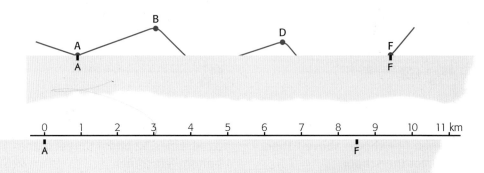

1	Lay the strip of paper on the map, to join points A and F.
2	Mark it at A and F.
3	Now lay the paper along the scale line to find the distance AF.

From A to F as the crow flies is 8.5 km.

2 By road

Roads bend and twist. So it is further from A to F by road than as the crow flies. This is how to measure it:

1	Lay the strip of paper along the straight section of road from A to B.
2	Mark it at A and B.
3	Pivot the paper at B until it lies along the next straight section, B to C. Mark it at C.
4	Now pivot it at C so that it lies along the next straight section, C to D. Mark it at D.
5	Move along the road in this way, section by section, until you reach F.
6	Place the paper along the scale line to find the distance AF.

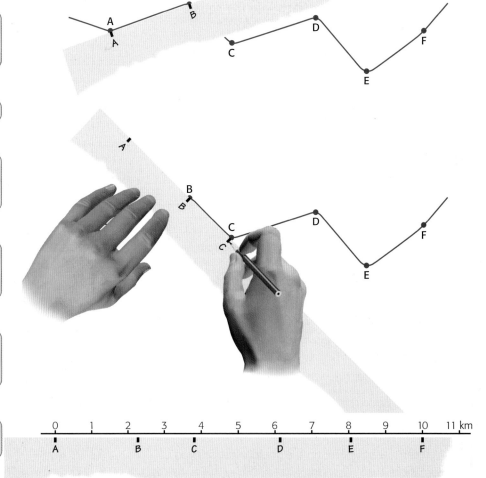

From A to F by road is 10 km

Your turn

The photo and map on page 14 showed part of the River Mole valley in Surrey. This map shows more of the same area. (What do you notice about the scale this time?)

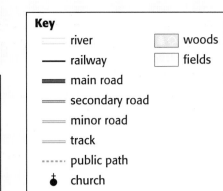

Key

═══ river	▨ woods
━━ railway	▢ fields
━━ main road	
═══ secondary road	
═══ minor road	
═══ track	
┈┈ public path	
♦ church	
☕ pub	
PO post office	
⦙⦙ raised bank (embankment)	
⊃⊂ bridge	
● railway station	

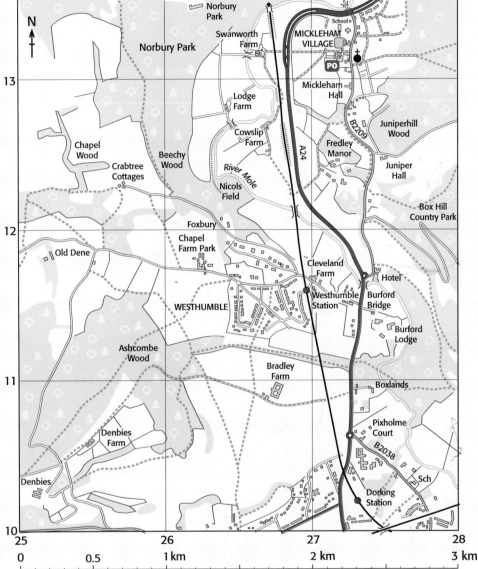

▲ Boxlands.

▲ Juniper Hall.

1 How far is it as the crow flies from Mickleham church to Westhumble station?

2 How far is it by rail from Westhumble station to Dorking station?

3 About how far is it by road from Mickleham Hall (273129) to the hotel at 274117?

4 Arthur hired a bike at Westhumble station. He followed these directions:
Go along the short road from the station to the T-junction at Cleveland Farm. Turn left. At the next fork, take the road to the left and cycle for 0.7 km.
Where did he end up?

5 Every day, Kim's mother collects her from school at 276103 and drives her home by this route:
From the school, go right on the B2038.
At the roundabout, take the A24 north for 0.9 km.
Turn left onto the minor road and continue for 0.5 km.
Now take the road to the right and continue for 1.4 km.
Where does Kim live?

6 Juniper Hall and Boxlands are shown above.
a Find them on the map, and give six-figure grid references for them.
b Write instructions telling a friend how to get from Juniper Hall to Boxlands. Don't forget distances!

17

Which direction ?

In this unit you will learn how to give and follow directions, using N, S, E and W.

The compass points

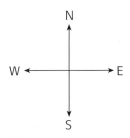

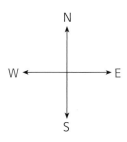

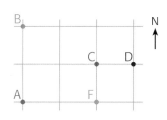

N, S, E, W are the four compass points: north, south, east, west.

Don't get east and west mixed up. Remember they form the word **we**.

Here B is north of A. F is east of A. C is west of D.

We can add other directions in between, like this:

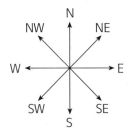

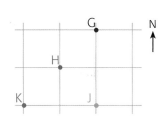

NE stands for north east (or north *of* east). SW stands for south west (or south *of* west).

Here, G is north east of H. J is south east of H. K is south west of H.

Did you know?

• You can use a compass to tell you where N is.
• The compass was invented in China.
• The first one was an iron needle floating in a bowl of water.

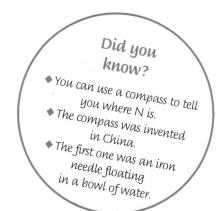

Your turn

1 You are standing at C in the first grid above. Which direction do you face when you turn towards:
 a F? b D? c A? d B?

2 Page 19 shows where Arthur went on holiday. The bowling alley is in square D5. What is in square:
 a A10? b F6? c C4? d F2?

3 You are at the hostel. In which direction is :
 a bike hire?
 b the riding school?

4 In which direction would you go, to get to:
 a the duck pond, from the pizza place?
 b the gym, from the bowling alley?
 c bike hire, from the kite shop?

5 How far is it by footpath from the door of the hostel to the door of the bike hire shop? You can use your ruler as a linear scale.

6 To get from the cafe to where Arthur stayed:
 ◆ From the cafe door, walk 50 m SE, then 65 m N.
 ◆ Next walk 40 m E, then 10 m SE, then 10 m SW.
 Where did he stay?

Treasure hunt

7 Look for the ● near the main gate. From here, if you go 2 squares N, then 1 square NW, you will arrive at the letter ⓐ.
Now follow the directions below, in order. For each, write down the letter you arrive at. The letters will make a word.
 ◆ Start at ●. Go 2 squares W.
 ◆ Then go 8 squares N and 4 squares E.
 ◆ Then go 1 square N and 5 squares W.
 ◆ Next, go 2 squares SE then 4 squares S.
 ◆ Then go 2 squares SW and 1 square SE.
 ◆ Then 3 squares NW, followed by 4 squares E, then 3 squares NE, then 2 squares N.
What word have you made?

8 a Now choose your own word, with at least 5 letters but not more than 8.
 b Write instructions for making this word, like those in question 7. Start from the ●.
 c Ask a partner to follow the instructions.

Map of your holiday village

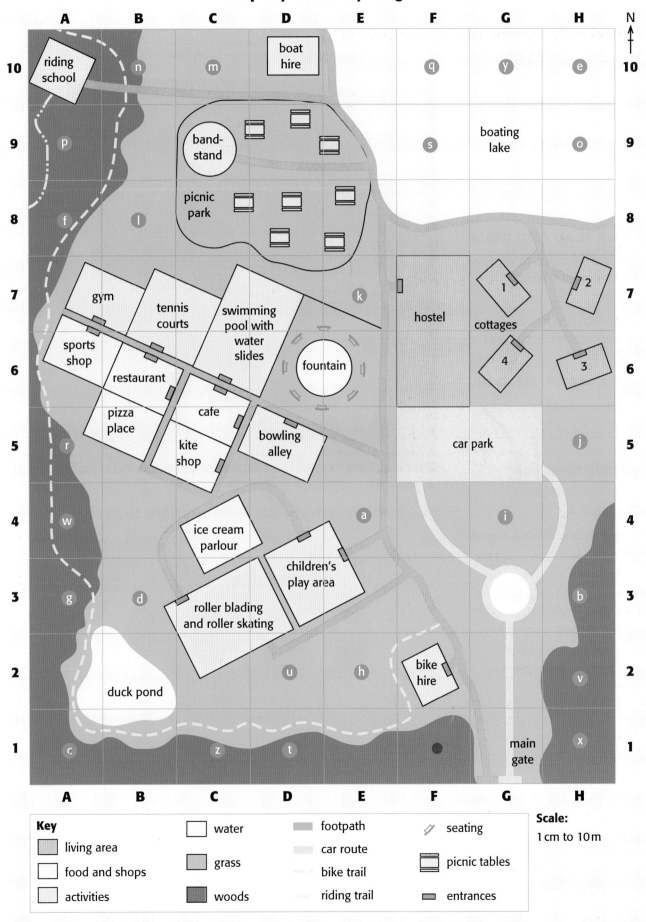

N

Key

living area	
food and shops	
activities	

water	
grass	
woods	

footpath	
car route	
bike trail	
riding trail	

seating	
picnic tables	
entrances	

Scale:
1 cm to 10 m

Drawing a sketch map

In this unit you'll learn about simple maps you can draw for yourself – sketch maps.

What's a sketch map?

A sketch map is a simple map to do a job – for example to show what a place is like, or how to get from one place to another.

A sketch map can be quite rough. If it does what you want, it's fine!

A sketch map of a place

This photo shows part of Warkworth in Northumberland, where Arthur's cousin Violet lives.

Look at the loop in the river, and the remains of the Norman castle.

And below is a sketch map of the same place, which Arthur started.

(You will have to do one later.)

A sketch map should have:

◆ a title, frame, and key

◆ an N arrow

◆ labels, and annotations (notes), where these help

◆ simple lines

◆ just enough detail to give a rough idea. (Don't show each building, or tree, or rock.)

Sketch maps are not to scale. You can add a note to say this.

all the open land outside the loop of the river is farmland

bridges

farmland

River Coquet

castle

Violet's house

▲ *Warkworth, from the air.*

Warkworth, where my cousin Violet lives. (Not to scale.)

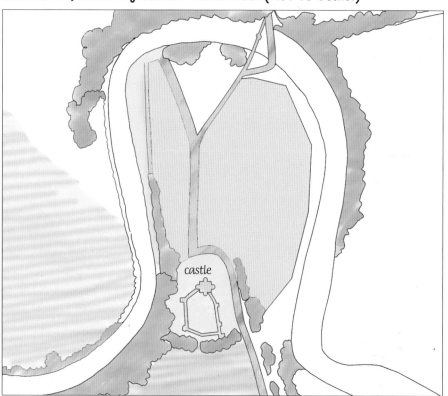

castle

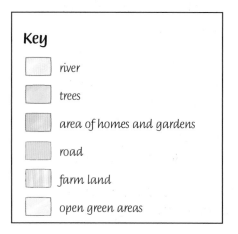

Key

	river
	trees
	area of homes and gardens
	road
	farm land
	open green areas

A sketch map to show a route

This street map shows Fort William, where Arthur lives. Find his house on it.

And below is a sketch map to show Arthur's route from his home to the post office.

The sketch map is not to scale. And it does not have much detail – just enough to be helpful.

Can you follow his route, on the street map?

▲ Arthur heads for the post office with a surprise for Violet.

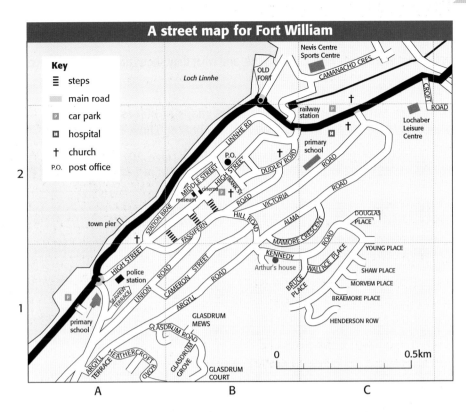

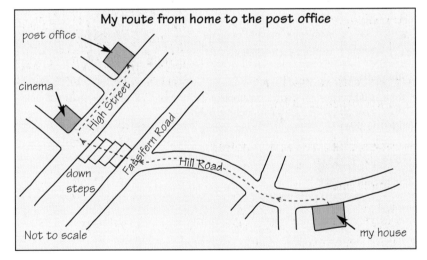

Your turn

1 Draw a sketch map (like the one Arthur started) for the photo on page 20. Don't forget a key!

2 Compare the street map and sketch map above.
   a Write down three differences between them.
   b Why was the cinema marked on the sketch map?

3 Look again at the street map. Arthur's house is on Kennedy Road, in square B1.
   a Work out a route from his house to the railway station.
   b Now draw a sketch map of the route. Show just enough detail to be helpful.
   c About how long is the route?

4 This is Arthur's route to his friend Gordon's house.
   ◆ Go out my front door, turn left.
   ◆ Take the second road on the left, and walk along it.
   ◆ When you reach the second road on the left, turn into it. Gordon's house is the first one on the right.
   a In which road does Gordon live?
   b In which direction is it from Arthur's house?
   c About how far is it from his house?

5 Compare the street map with the map on page 14.
   a The grid lines are labelled differently. In what way?
   b Which grid system do you think is simpler to use?
   c Which lets you be more precise? Why?

Ordnance Survey maps

In this unit you'll learn what OS maps are, and what they show, and how to use them.

What are OS maps?

Ordnance Survey maps or **OS maps** are maps of places. They are to scale, and give lots of detail. They use symbols to show things.

The OS map opposite shows Warkworth (from page 20), and Amble. The key below has the symbols. (And there's a larger key on page 126.)

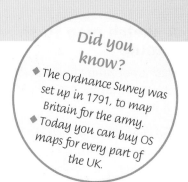

Did you know?
- The Ordnance Survey was set up in 1791, to map Britain for the army.
- Today you can buy OS maps for every part of the UK.

Key

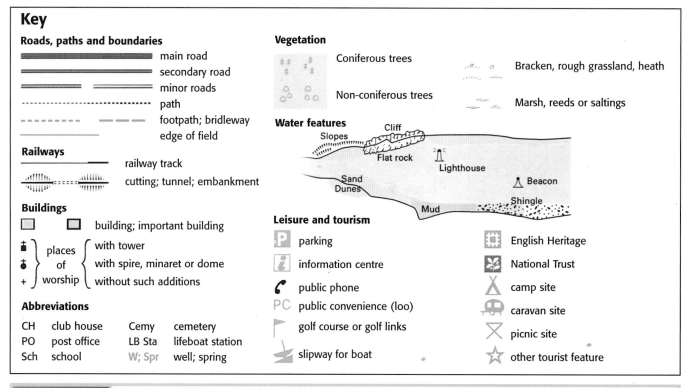

Roads, paths and boundaries
- main road
- secondary road
- minor roads
- path
- footpath; bridleway
- edge of field

Railways
- railway track
- cutting; tunnel; embankment

Buildings
- building; important building
- places of worship { with tower / with spire, minaret or dome / without such additions }

Abbreviations
CH	club house	Cemy	cemetery
PO	post office	LB Sta	lifeboat station
Sch	school	W; Spr	well; spring

Vegetation
- Coniferous trees
- Non-coniferous trees
- Bracken, rough grassland, heath
- Marsh, reeds or saltings

Water features
Slopes, Cliff, Flat rock, Lighthouse, Sand Dunes, Beacon, Mud, Shingle

Leisure and tourism
- P parking
- i information centre
- public phone
- PC public convenience (loo)
- golf course or golf links
- slipway for boat
- English Heritage
- National Trust
- camp site
- caravan site
- picnic site
- other tourist feature

Your turn

1 Look at Warkworth on the OS map. Name the river that flows through it. Where is it flowing to?

2 What signs can you find that Warkworth is a historic place? List them. (There are three!)

3 What is at this grid reference, in Warkworth?
   a 247057   b 247062
   c 249063   d 247052

4 The top of an OS map is always north. Look back at the photo of Warkworth on page 20. Where on the photo is north?

5 Violet's house is in the lower right corner of the photo on page 20. Find it. Then find it on the OS map and write a six-figure grid reference for it.

6 Warkworth has a population of 1600. Now look at Amble. Which of these is its population?
   a 1000   b 2000   c 5600   d 9300
   How did you decide?

7 How many of these are there in Amble?
   a schools   b places of worship   c cemeteries

8 Find one of these on the map and give a six-figure grid reference for it:
   a a post office   b a club house
   c a public phone box   d a mast

9 What clues are there on the map that Warkworth and Amble get lots of visitors? Give as many as you can.

10 What is there for tourists to do, around Warkworth and Amble? Using the information on the map, write a list.

11 On the map, what clues are there that the coast and sea around Amble might be dangerous?

12 Violet used to go to the school in square 2503.
   a How far is it from her home? (Use the scale.)
   b Pretend you are Violet. Draw a sketch map of your route to the school. Mark in what you think are the key things you see on the way.

Scale 1: 25 000

0   0.5   1 km   2 km   3 km

How high?

St Andrews

In this unit you'll learn how height is shown on an OS map.

A hilly problem

This aerial photo shows Kellie Castle, which is in a hamlet called Arncroach:
That is near St Andrews, where Arthur's uncle Iain lives.

From the photo, you can't tell if the area is hilly, or high up.
But below is an OS map of the same area. This tells you a lot about the
height, and hills. In two different ways …

▲ *Kellie Castle, at Arncroach in Fife.*

0   0.25   0.5   0.75   1 km

1 **Contour lines.** Everywhere along a contour line is the same height above sea level. The number on the line shows the height in metres. The contour lines on this map are at 5m intervals.

2 **Spot heights.** They give the exact height at a spot, in metres above sea level.

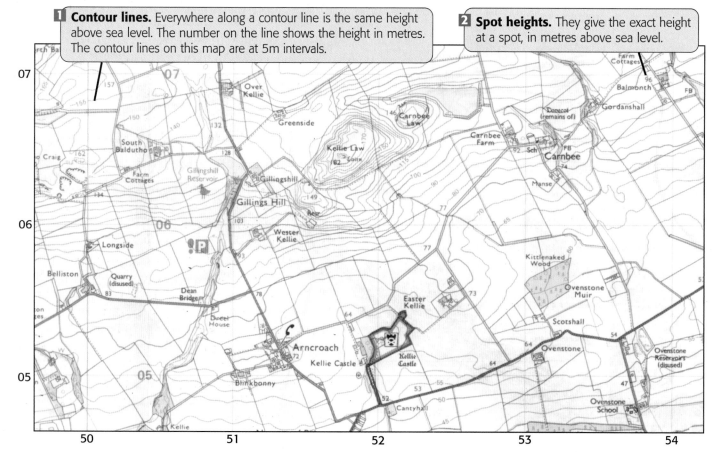

More about contour lines

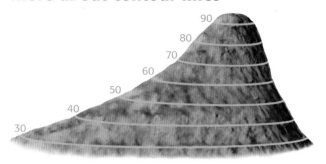

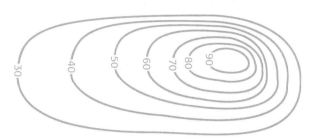

The contour lines are marked on this hill at 10 metre intervals. On a map, you see them from above …

… like this. They are close together where the slope is steep, and further apart where it is gentle.

Remember:

◆ where contour lines are very far apart, it means the ground is flat.

◆ where they are very close together, the ground slopes steeply.

Did you know?

◆ *The highest place in the UK is Ben Nevis (1344 m).*
◆ *Some places in the UK are below sea level! (Check the map on page 127.)*

Your turn

1 Match the drawings to the contour lines.
   Start your answer like this: **A =**

   A
   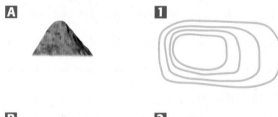

   1

   B
   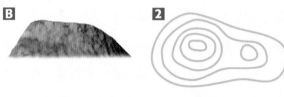

   2

   C

   3

The following questions refer to the OS map.

2 First, the map has lots of thin black lines everywhere. What do you think they show? (The key won't help!)

3 a Find the contour line labelled 65, on the right hand side of the map. What does the 65 tell you?
   b What number is on the line below it?
   c Follow the '65' contour line with your finger, to find a building that is about 65 m above sea level. Give its name, and four-figure grid reference.

4 About how high above sea level is:
   a Dreel House (5005)? b Carnbree Farm (5206)?

5 a Which full square on the map has the steepest land? How can you tell?
   b Which has the flattest land? How did you decide?

6 Walking by road or footpath (dashed line) say whether it is uphill, downhill, or along nearly flat land:
   a from Arncroach (5105) to Gillingshill (5106)
   b from Blinkbonny (5104) to Arncroach (5105)
   c from Gillingshill (5106) to Carnbee school (5306)
   d from Belliston (4905) to Dean Bridge (5005)
   e from Scotshall (5305) to Ovenstone School (5304)

7 Find the stream to the west of Over Kellie, in square 5006. Which way is it flowing, towards the north or towards the south? Give your evidence.

8 a The highest point on the map is shown by a spot height. Find it, and give its six-figure grid reference.
   b There is a historic feature at this point. What is it? (Glossary?) And why do you think they built it here?

9 Some spot heights are shown in orange on the map, and some in black. What's the difference? (Page 126?)

10 Now, find Kellie Castle on the map.
   a What does the purple outline tell you?
   b You are at Gillingshill. A tourist asks you how to get from there to Kellie Castle. Write down what you will say, and give rough distances. (The entrance to the castle is shown by the two long purple lines.)

11 a Choose two other places on the map, next to roads.
   b Write instructions for getting from one to the other, by car. Give distances.
   c Give the instructions to your partner to follow – but name *only* the start point. Does your partner reach the correct end point?

Latitude and longitude

Here you will learn what latitude and longitude are, and how to look them up.

Where on Earth?

The Earth is like a big round ball. So how do you say where a place is, on a ball? Easy! Cover the ball with grid lines, like the map on page 14.

The two main grid lines

Look at drawing **A**. It shows the Earth with its two main grid lines:
– the **equator** goes around the middle of the Earth, like a belt
– the **prime meridian** circles it from north to south.

So now you can say that the UK is north of the equator, and most of it is west of the prime meridian. (In fact the prime meridian passes through Greenwich in London.)

Lines of latitude and longitude

Now look at drawing **B**. This time more grid lines have been added. They will help you to tell more exactly where a place is.

The lines going across are called **lines of latitude**. They tell you how far a place is north or south of the equator, in **degrees (°)**.

The lines from north to south are **lines of longitude**. They tell you how far a place is east or west of the prime meridian, in degrees.

A closer look

Now look at drawing **C**. It shows part of **B**, enlarged. You can see that the lines of latitude and longitude have degrees marked on them.

So the British Isles lies between 50° and 61° north of the equator. And between 2° east and 11° west of the prime meridian. What can you say about Aberdeen's position?

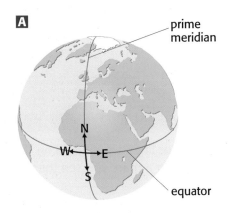

A

prime meridian

equator

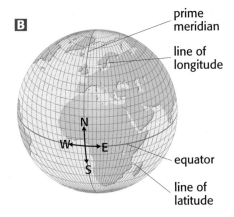

B

prime meridian

line of longitude

equator

line of latitude

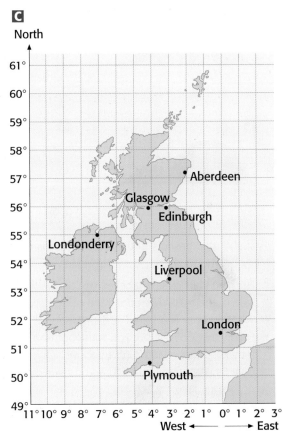

C

◀ *East meets West! The line marks the prime meridian, at the Greenwich Observatory in London.*

Getting even closer

Now, a challenge. You want to say more *exactly* where Glasgow is, on the Earth. How can you do that? Like this:

◆ Divide a degree into 60 equal parts, called minutes, in your mind. **1 degree = 60 minutes** or **60′.**

◆ Then give the latitude and longitude of Glasgow in degrees and minutes. (It is a bit like giving 6-figure grid references.)

Look at drawing **D**. It has a grey line at every tenth minute. Using these lines to help us, we can say that Glasgow is:

    55° and 50′ north of the equator (or 55 50N)
    4° and 15′ west of the prime meridian (or 4 15W)

These numbers are called the **co-ordinates** for Glasgow. It is the only place on the Earth with these co-ordinates.

Every place on the Earth has its own co-ordinates.

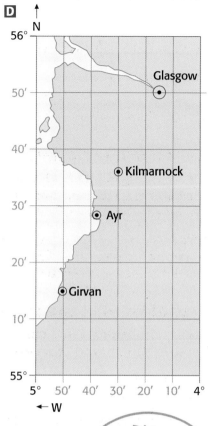

Looking up an atlas

If you look in the back of an atlas, you will find an index of places. If you look up Ayr, you may find something like this:

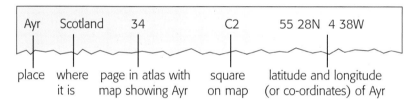

Ayr	Scotland	34	C2	55 28N 4 38W

place   where   page in atlas with   square   latitude and longitude
         it is   map showing Ayr   on map   (or co-ordinates) of Ayr

Now look at Ayr on the map above. Does it match those atlas co-ordinates?

Did you know?
◆ *The prime meridian crosses the equator at two places.*
◆ *One is in the Atlantic Ocean, the other in the Pacific Ocean.*

Your turn

1 What does this term mean? (The glossary may help.)
  a equator   **b** prime meridian
  c latitude   **d** longitude

2 Using the map on page 26, give a rough latitude and longitude (in degrees but no minutes) for:
  a Edinburgh
  b Plymouth
  c Londonderry

3 Using the map at the top of this page, name the place at:
  a 55 15N 4 51W   **b** 55 36N 4 30W

4 Now turn to the map of the British Isles on page 127. See if you can name the city at:
  a 52 30N 1 50W   **b** 51 30N 3 13W
  c 55 59N 3 13W   **d** 52 58N 1 10W

5 Using the map on page 127, see if you can give the latitude and longitude (in degrees and minutes) of:
  a Bristol   **b** Aberdeen   **c** Leeds
  d where you live (if hasn't been mentioned yet!)

You will need an atlas for questions **6** and **7**.

6 Using the atlas index to help you, make a table showing latitude and longitude for 8 capital cities around the world. Start like this:

Country	Capital	Latitude and longitude
England		

7

	Country	City	Latitude and longitude
i	Egypt	?	30 03N 31 15E
ii	Finland	?	60 08N 25 00E
iii	Turkey	?	41 02N 28 57E
iv	Peru	?	5 15S 80 38W
v	?	?	?

  a A challenge! Using the atlas maps to help you, name the missing cities in rows **i** to **iv**.
  b Pick a fifth city so that the first letters of the 5 cities make a word. Give the missing information for it.

The big picture

This chapter is about settlements – the villages and towns and cities we live in.

These are the big ideas behind the chapter:

- Humans like us first appeared on the Earth about 200 000 years ago, and began to spread all over it.
- As they explored it, they found places they wanted to settle in.
- They started by building shelters. Over time, these grew into villages, and towns, and cities.
- Today, our settlements are still growing, and still changing.

Your goals for this chapter

By the end of this chapter you should be able to answer these questions:

- What factors did our ancestors think about, in choosing a place to settle in?
- What do these terms mean?

  settlement   site   situation

- What kinds of things cause a settlement to grow?
- What kind of pattern do settlements tend to follow, as they grow?
- What can an OS map tell me, about land use in a town or city?
- What do these terms mean?

  urban area   rural area   redevelopment
  urban regeneration   greenfield   brownfield

- In what ways might land use change over time?
- What does *sustainable development* mean, and what examples can I give?

And then …

When you finish the chapter, come back to this page and see if you have met your goals!

Did you know?
- Northumberland has the remains of a house nearly 10 000 years old.
- It's a shallow pit, which still had traces of ancient meals (including nutshells) !

Did you know?
- By 2005, there were 25 megacities – cities with over 10 million people !

Did you know?
- Villages did not start to form until humans had learned to farm.

Did you know?
- The settlement called London was started by the Romans, around 50 AD.
- We think its name means 'the settlement on the wide river'.

Your chapter starter

Page 28 shows a settlement.

What's a settlement?

Pick out five key things you notice about this one.

Do you think it has always looked like this? Give your reasons.

In what ways is your settlement like this one? In what ways is it different?

Settle down, you lot!

Settling down

In this unit you'll find out what we humans looked for, when choosing a place to settle in.

Once upon a time

The Earth was empty for billions of years. But life evolved. And around 200 000 years ago …

… the first humans appeared. They lived by eating fruit and berries, hunting, fishing …

… which meant they were nearly always on the move, chasing dinner.

Then, one day, they noticed something amazing: where they dropped seeds, plants grew!

So they began to settle down in one place and grow their food. These were the first farmers.

They chose a place or **site** that had what they needed. Like good flat land … water … wood for fuel …

… shelter from wind and rain … materials for making things (clay, stone, wood, tin …) …

… easy access to other places for trading … and protection from their enemies.

They cleared the land and planted crops and put up dwellings. The result – a **settlement**.

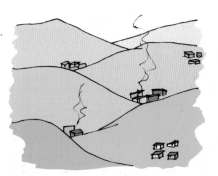

Years passed. The numbers of humans – and settlements – grew.

Some settlements grew larger and larger. And now …

… there are over 6 billion humans, and half of us live in cities.

Your turn

1 It is 5000 BC. You are leading your tribe on a search for a place to settle in. Draw a spider map showing the factors you will consider, when choosing a site – like this:

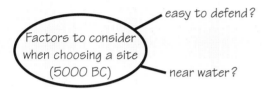

easy to defend?

Factors to consider when choosing a site (5000 BC)

near water?

2 Copy and complete in your own words:
   a A settlement is …
   b A site is …
   c The *situation* of a settlement means …
   The glossary may help.

3 Look at the photos **A** to **E**. For each photo, decide whether it shows a settlement or not. Give your reasons.

4 For each *settlement* in the photos, suggest reasons for choosing that site. (Try for at least two reasons for each.)

5 The five photos were taken in the countries listed below. Try to match each photo to the correct country.
   Switzerland   Morocco   The Philippines
   France   Canada

6 The government wants to build a new town in the UK, starting next year.
   a What factors do you think will be important, when choosing a site for it? List them, and say why they are important.
   b Underline any factors that did *not* apply in 5000 BC.

A

B

C

D

E

Example: settling in Aberdeen

Here you'll learn about the early settlements that became Aberdeen city.

Once upon a time

By 12 500 years ago, the thick ice that had covered Scotland, and most of the British Isles, had melted. Forests began to appear, and wild animals. Wolves, bear, deer, bison, lynx and wild boar roamed the land.

And then, humans. They came from the mainland of Europe. First as hunters, and then they began to farm.

The early settlers around Aberdeen

People have lived in the area that is now Aberdeen for at least 8000 years. We know this from the hundreds of clues they left behind.

The map below shows how the area looked around 1660. There were two settlements, Aberdeen and Old Aberdeen. Aberdeen was an important Royal Burgh, with trading links across Europe. Old Aberdeen was centred around a cathedral and a college. Their total population may have been about 9000.

But over time, the settlements grew, and joined, and spread, to become Aberdeen city. The red dashed line shows the city limits today.

Look at the photos. They show some of the clues from Aberdeen's past. Match them to the dots on the map, to see where they were found.

One of the many hoards of silver coins found in Aberdeen city centre. They date from 700 – 800 years ago. The people of Aberdeen looked after their money carefully!

This is Standingstones stone circle. It was built by the early farmers for their ceremonies, 4000 – 5000 years ago. The tallest stone is 3.3 metres high.

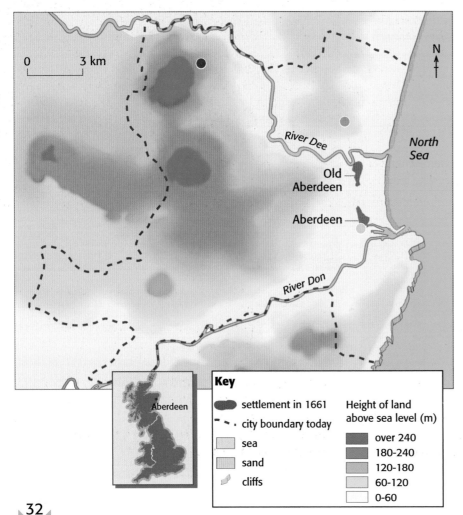

This man lived around 4000 years ago. His stone 'coffin' was found in 1975, during building work. There may have been a drink, for the afterlife, in the pottery bowl.

Key

settlement in 1661	Height of land above sea level (m)
city boundary today	
sea	over 240
sand	180-240
cliffs	120-180
	60-120
	0-60

Then and now

The map below was drawn in 1661 by a parson called James Gordon. It shows the two settlements you saw on the last map.

The town council gave him a silver cup, a silk hat, and a silk gown for his wife, as pay.

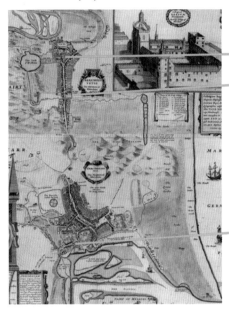

Now look at the yellow lines. They link buildings on his map with the same buildings you can still see (but with many changes) today.

The top line is for St Machar's Cathedral, which dates from 1370. The next is for King's College, which dates from 1500. And the lowest line is for St Nicholas Kirk, which dates from before 1151.

And this shows just *part* of Aberdeen today. It has grown rather a lot! The dots match those on the map on page 32.

Your turn

1 Look at the map on page 32.
Why do you think people chose those two places to settle in? Give as many reasons as you can.

2 Aberdeen was a trading centre, with trading links across Europe. What advantages do you think it had over Old Aberdeen, for trading? The OS map on page 37 may help. (Look at the coastline and the river mouths.)

3 About how many times larger is the city today (the red dashed line) than the two early settlements together?
About: a 60 times b 170 times c 310 times

4 See if you can think up a way to get a more accurate answer for question 3.

5 It is 1660. You are James Gordon. The council has asked you to draw a map of Old Aberdeen and Aberdeen. How will you go about it?

6 It is today – and you are still James Gordon! You have arrived from the past in a time pod. You are amazed by what you see around you.
Write a letter to your wife telling her what Aberdeen is like now, and how you feel about it.

How settlements grow

In this unit you'll learn why some settlements grow – with Aberdeen as example.

A good choice?

In the last two units you saw how new arrivals chose a place to settle. If the site is a good one, the settlement will grow. Like this …

They'll likely be wanting a guid baker!

My jings, wife!

And then I'll build a factory round it.

But it's just steam, Willie!

Will they gie us oor denner?

People hear it's a good place, and come looking for work – for example as bakers and tailors.

The population also grows naturally – but quite slowly – through birth.

Then, around 1750, the Industrial Revolution starts in the UK. Many settlements now start …

… to grow fast, because people flock in from the countryside to work in the new factories.

In this way, small settlements grow into villages, then towns, then cities.

Advantages that helped Aberdeen grow

Old Aberdeen and Aberdeen had some big natural advantages, that helped them grow, and grow, and grow. (Look back at the last unit.)

For the early settlers …

◆ There were two fine rivers for fresh water, and for travel inland by boat. There were also many smaller streams.

◆ The rivers were rich in salmon. Tasty!

◆ The settlements were on the coast. So people could trade by sea with many places, including England and other parts of Europe.

◆ Coast meant sea fishing – and a good place to build boats.

◆ There was plenty of wood around for boat building. (But later, boats would need iron.)

◆ The area had good farmland. It had plenty of rain, so grass grew well. Farmers reared cattle for meat and milk, and sheep for meat and wool. They brought these to the market in Aberdeen to sell.

And later …

◆ Later the running water would be used to power textile mills, and give water for steam engines, and many industries.

◆ The local rock was granite. It grew popular for building – and for tombstones. It was sent by sea to London and other places.

◆ Oil and gas were discovered not too far away, in the North Sea.

The local area did not have coal, or iron ore, for its industry. Aberdeen had to get these from other places. But that did not stop it growing!

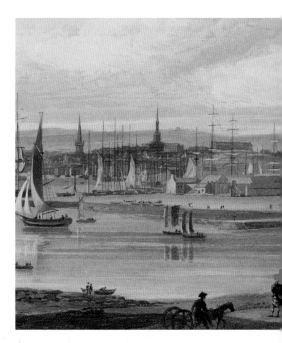

▲ *The busy port of Aberdeen, around 1820 (nearly 200 years ago).*

Aberdeen gets busy ...

This table shows events that helped Aberdeen to grow.

Which ones are linked to its natural advantages?

Did you know?
● Aberdeen used to be famous for envelopes!

Events that helped Aberdeen to grow

Year	Event
1749	A new linen mill opens
1753	The first two whaling ships leave Aberdeen, to catch whales for oil (for lamps)
1760	Around now, Aberdeen granite starts to be used for pavements in London
1789	A new woollen mill opens (so by now there are lots of textile mills)
1790	A big new shipyard opens, to build sailing ships; later it will build steam ships
1805	A new canal opens, linking Aberdeen to Inverurie
1807	A big new paper mill opens (by now Aberdeen has several)
1850	First of the railway lines from Aberdeen opens (going towards Forfar)
1882	First of Aberdeen's steam-driven fishing trawlers built
1889	Large new fish market opens; Aberdeen is now an important fishing centre
1934	Aberdeen airport opens
1965	By now food processing is becoming important (of bacon, meat, fish)
1965	Gas discovered in the North Sea
1969	Oil discovered in the North Sea; Aberdeen becomes a base for exploration

Your turn

1 Its natural advantages helped Aberdeen to grow.
   a Make a table for Aberdeen, starting like this:

Natural advantage	Jobs linked to this
good farmland around it	farmer
	wool weaver

   b In the first column list its natural advantages.
   c In the second, list jobs linked to each advantage. Give as many as you can.
   d Which natural advantage do you think has been the most important one, for Aberdeen? Give reasons.

2 In Unit 3.2 you saw how Aberdeen has grown in area. This graph shows how it has grown in population:

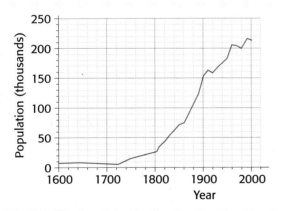

   a About what was the population in the year:
      i 1600?   ii 1800?   iii 2000?
   b About how many times larger was the population in 2000 than in 1600?
   c i In which period did it grow fastest?
         1700 – 1800   1800 – 1900   1900 – 2000
      ii Explain why, using information given in this unit.

3 Explain why each of these helped Aberdeen to grow:
   a the new woollen mill, opened in 1749
   b the building of fishing trawlers, from 1882
   c the airport, opened in 1934
   d the discovery of North Sea oil, in 1969

4 Industries can be divided into three types: *primary*, *secondary*, and *tertiary*.
   a Find out what each term in italics means. (Glossary!)
   b Using the information in this unit, see if you can give two examples of each type of industry, for Aberdeen.

5 Industries rise – and then **decline** over time. Look at this simplified graph:

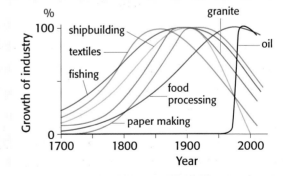

   a What does *decline* mean? (Glossary?)
   b Which industry has completely declined, in Aberdeen?
   c Which are still quite important today?
   d i Which one grew the most rapidly? Why was this?
      ii Do you think it will ever die away? Explain.

6 Arthur lives in Fort William. It is also on the coast. But its population is only 10 000. Why did it not grow like Aberdeen? See if you can think up some reasons.

Land use in towns and cities

In this unit you'll learn about the pattern settlements usually follow, as they grow.

As a settlement grows …

As a settlement grows, things like shops and homes and factories group in areas that have **advantages** for them. So a pattern develops.

◆ A settlement starts small – perhaps a few dwellings and a workshop.

◆ As it grows, it spreads out in all directions: along the roads that lead into it, then filling in between them.

◆ As it grows, the older part where it started, and where the roads meet, gets taken over by shops and offices. They have an advantage here: people can reach them from all directions.

◆ This area of shops and offices becomes the **central business district** or **CBD**. The land grows more expensive here, because so many want it.

◆ As the settlement grows, new houses are usually built around the edge of it, where there is more space and land is cheaper.

◆ In the old days, factories were built along canals, rivers or railways, so that goods could be moved easily – and some needed lots of water.

◆ Modern factories are built close to major roads, because most goods get moved by road – and towards the outskirts where land is cheaper.

Clues from an OS map

◆ Look for the area of the town or city that seems the most built-up and central, and where the roads meet or **converge**. This is the CBD.

◆ Look around the edge of the town or city for modern housing estates, with more open space around them.

◆ Industrial areas are marked **Industrial Estate**. Some old factories are marked **Works**. You may find high tech companies such as mobile phone companies in a **Business Park** or **Technology Park**.

Now study these photos from Aberdeen, then try 'Your turn'.

New industrial area
New **industrial estates** and **business parks** are built near the edge of the town or city where land is cheaper, and near main roads for easy access.

Old industrial area
This one is along a canal, but you will find them along rivers and railways too. Many old factories are now closed. The area may look run down.

Modern housing
New houses and housing estates are towards the edge of town. There may be parks, golf clubs, and new shopping areas nearby.

Older housing
Near the CBD and old industrial areas, you may find 19th century housing like this, built cheaply for the workers. It may be 'done up' by now.

The CBD
Here you will find busy streets, banks, big department stores, airline offices, cafes, restaurants, and perhaps a cathedral, museum, cinema, theatre.

In general, as you move out from the CBD:
◆ land gets cheaper to buy or rent
◆ housing gets more modern.

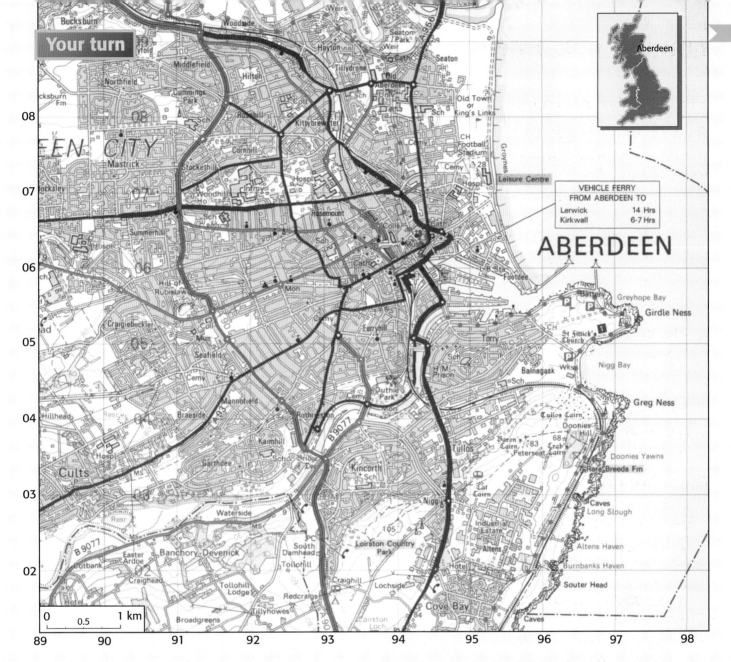

1 Look at the OS map of Aberdeen, above.
   What do the shapes like this ▭ represent?

2 a What do the letters **CBD** stand for?
   b Photo **A** shows the CBD. Which of these squares do
     you think contains the main part of the CBD?
     i 9103   **ii** 9204   **iii** 9305   **iv** 9306
     Explain your choice.

3 As you saw on page 32, Aberdeen grew from *two*
   small settlements, Old Aberdeen and Aberdeen.
   a Old Aberdeen is marked on the OS map above.
     Which squares is it in? (Look near the top right.)
   b Which squares correspond to the other settlement?
     Use the map on page 32 to help you decide.
   c Can you see any link between the settlement in **b**
     and today's CBD? Explain what you notice.

4 The old textile factory in photo D is now closed down.
   It is in square 9306, in an old industrial area. What
   advantages would this area have had, for factories?

5 One of the houses shown in photos A and B is in
   square 9506. Which one do you think it is? Explain
   why you think so.

6 Many roads converge on the CBD.
   a What problems might this cause?
   b Why was the major road (shown in green) built?

7 Most of the land in Aberdeen is used for houses,
   industry, shops and offices. But some has other uses.
   a Make a table with these headings:

Other types of land use in Aberdeen		
transport	leisure	other
roads		

   b In your table, write in all the other types of land use
     you can find on the map.

8 And finally, turn to the aerial photo of Aberdeen on
   page 32. Pick out three things on it. Then find these
   on the map above, and give grid references for them.

Change around town: Edinburgh Quay

Here you'll see an example of how land use changes over time.

All change around the Lochrin basin

The photo on the right was taken in 2006. It shows the Fountainbridge area in Edinburgh, near the city centre, where the Union Canal starts.

The canal was opened in 1822. Its main purpose was to bring coal, granite, slate, limestone and other materials into Edinburgh. (It carried many passengers too.)

In time the railway, and then trucks, took over, for moving goods around. And in 1965 the canal was officially closed. Much of the area around it became run down.

But in 2002, exciting changes came to the Lochrin basin. The canal was drained (above) and cleaned up. Run-down buildings were removed. New building work started.

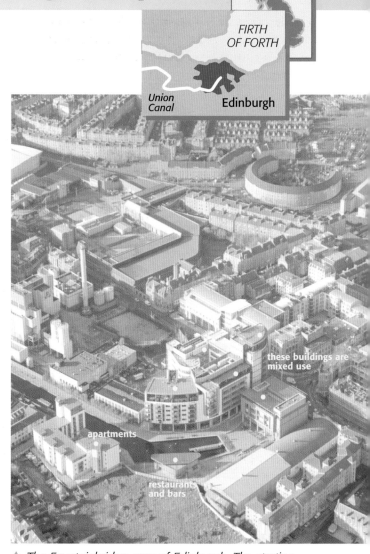

▲ The Fountainbridge area of Edinburgh. The starting point of the canal is called the Lochrin basin.
The buildings marked by yellow dots are the Edinburgh Quay development.

The result is Edinburgh Quay, a smart development with offices, restaurants and apartments. And a clean canal, with canal boats again on the water.

38

Who did it?

A body called British Waterways is responsible for looking after the UK's canals. For the work on the Lochrin Basin they teamed up with a **developer**.

The project cost a lot: £60 million. But the offices, apartments, and restaurants are being rented out, and will give a profit over the years.

The benefits

The development brings many benefits:

◆ up to 650 jobs, in the new offices and restaurants

◆ a canalside, close to the city centre, that is now an attractive place to visit – and live

◆ an area that was badly neglected brought to life again. That's always good to see!

A successful development attracts others. And now there are several other projects planned for the area.

It's part of a much bigger plan!

The development at the Lochrin basin is part of a much bigger project that aims to transform not only this area, but a large part of central Scotland.

It is called the **Millennium Canal Link** and you can find out about it in the next unit.

▼ *Part of the OS map of Edinburgh. Find Fountainbridge on it. Can you see any historic buildings not too far away?*

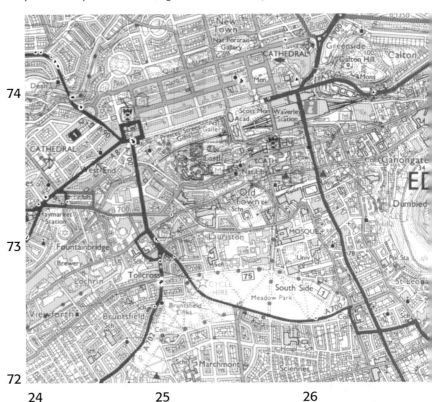

Did you know?

◆ *The Union canal is a* **contour canal** *– all at the same height above sea level.*

Your turn

1 Compare the aerial photo on page 38 with the OS map above.

  a Find the Lochrin basin on the OS map, and give a six-figure grid reference for the very end of the canal.

  b Now work out which compass direction the camera was pointing in, for the aerial photo.

2 Look again at the photo. With the help of the map, identify what the land is being used for, in the Fountainbridge area. Write a list of land uses.

3 Now the site at Edinburgh Quay is being used for offices, restaurants and apartments.

  a Do you think it may have had any of those uses 150 years ago, when the canal was still being used to transport goods (and people)?

  b What other uses may it have had, 150 years ago?

4 *Some of the area was derelict, and has been redeveloped.* Write that sentence in words that an 8-year-old could understand. (Glossary?)

5 The development is on a *brownfield site*.

  a What does the term in italics mean?

  b Now look in the glossary to find a term that means the opposite. (Hint: it starts with g!)

6 You run a design company with 12 staff, about 8 km from Edinburgh city centre. You plan to move your company to Edinburgh Quay.

Write a memo to your staff telling them about your plan, and the new offices, and why you think they will like it there.

7 Overall, do you think developments like Edinburgh Quay are a good idea? Write a letter to the editor of *The Edinburgh Echo* giving your opinion, and reasons.

Edinburgh to Glasgow - by canal!

Here you'll find out about the Millennium Canal Link – and what sustainable development means.

Scotland's Lowland canals

In June 1768, work began on an exciting new project: a canal right across Scotland, from the Atlantic Ocean to the North Sea.

22 years later the canal was complete, and ready for transporting goods. It was called the Forth & Clyde canal. It linked Glasgow to the Forth, as you can see on the map below.

Edinburgh wanted a canal too – mainly to bring coal and limestone from inland Scotland. So in 1818 work started on the Union canal, to link Edinburgh to the Forth & Clyde. It opened four years later.

Goods could be moved quite quickly along the canals. So they gave a big boost to Scottish industry. But then the railways came along. The canals could not compete. They closed down, and fell into neglect.

▲ A boat at the western end of the Forth & Clyde canal, in 1906.

The Millenium Canal link project

To mark the new Millennium in Scotland, they hit on a plan to restore and reopen the two canals. The project was completed in 2002. And now you can go from Edinburgh to Glasgow once more, by canal. Look at this map:

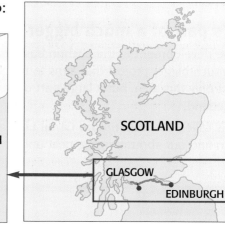

▲ The canals that link Edinburgh and Glasgow.

But it's only the start!

The Millenium Canal Link cost over £80 million. This was not spent for fun. The aim is to use the canals to help all the places that lie along them:

▲ *Party time: the opening of the new canal basin at Port Dundas in Glasgow, in September 2006, as part of the Millennium Canal Link project.*

So – is it sustainable development?

A change or development is **sustainable**, if:

◆ it benefits people socially, and …

◆ it benefits them economically, and …

◆ it benefits the environment (which includes the air, water and wildlife).

Sustainable development will not harm people, or the environment, in the present or the future.

So is the Millennium Canal Link project an example of sustainable development? What do you think?

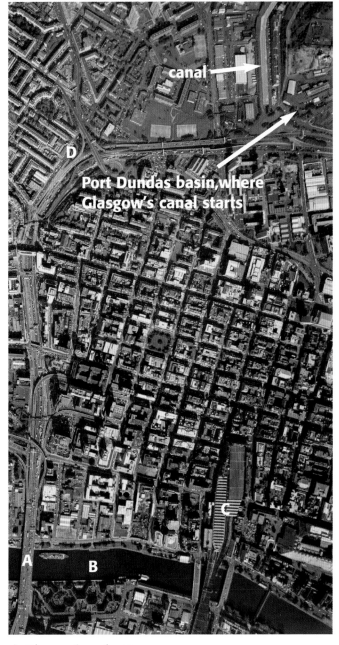

▲ *Glasgow from the air.*

Your turn

1 Around 1760, Glasgow was really keen to have a canal to link it to the Firth of Forth. Why do you think that was? (Page 129 may help.)

2 Edinburgh's reasons for wanting a canal were a bit different from Glasgow's. See if you can explain why.

3 a Look at the plans for development along the Millennium Canal Link. Pick out:
   i two social benefits
   ii two economic benefits
   iii two environmental benefits
   b Can you think of anything harmful about the plans?

4 a Overall, would you say the Millennium Canal Link project is an example of sustainable development?
  b Do you think it was a good choice, to celebrate the new millennium? Give your reasons.

5 Now look at the aerial photo of Glasgow.
  a Does the canal start out in the city suburbs, or in a fairly central location? What is your evidence?
  b What kind of buildings might you expect to find along the canal? Explain your answer.
  c Now look at the structures marked A – D above. What do you think they are?

Exploring your island home

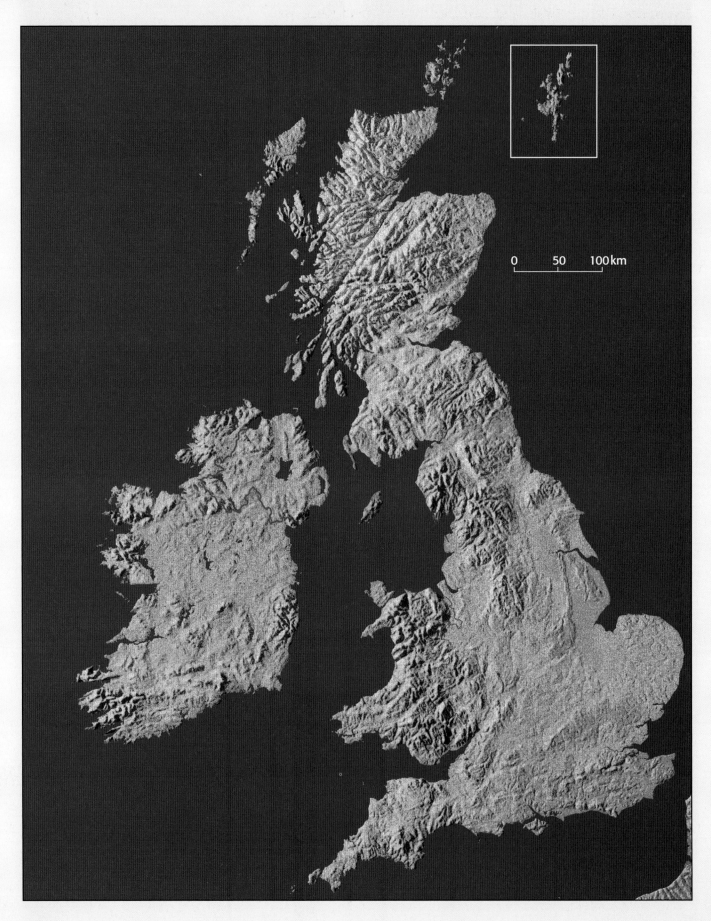

0   50   100 km

The big picture

This chapter is about Britain, and especially about Scotland, where you live. These are the big ideas behind the chapter:

- Britain has been shaped and changed by natural and human processes. This is still going on today.
- We think that humans began to settle here about 10 000 years ago, when the ice melted at the end of an Ice Age.
- We have spread all over Britain – farming it, mining it, building over it.
- We have also carved it up like a jigsaw, into different regions.
- It is a place of contrasts. Some parts are colder and wetter than others. Some are more crowded. Some are more wealthy.

Your goals for this chapter

By the end of this chapter you should be able to answer these questions:

- Which countries and nations make up the British Isles?
- What do these terms mean?
  the UK   Great Britain   Britain
- What are the main physical features of Britain?
- What kind of climate do we have?
- Which parts of the UK are the most crowded? And least crowded?
- What do these terms mean?
  urban area   rural area   population density
- Which are the UK's ten biggest cities, and where are they?
- What kinds of work do people in the UK do?
- What do these terms mean?
  economic activity   primary sector   secondary sector tertiary sector   services   manufacturing   industry
- Which parts of the UK are wealthiest, and which are poorest?
- What and where are Scotland's National Parks? And what are they like?

And then …

When you finish the chapter, come back to this page and see if you have met your goals!

Did you know?
- Around 200 million years ago, dinosaurs roamed Scotland.

Did you know?
- The British Isles has over 6000 islands. (Many are tiny.)

Did you know?
- Millions of years ago, Scotland had lots of volcanoes.
- Arthur's Seat in Edinburgh is the remains of one.

Did you know?
- Until about 8000 years ago, the British Isles were joined to the rest of Europe. (So you could walk to France!)
- But then they got cut off by rising seas, and floods.

Your chapter starter

Always happy to help.

Look at page 42. Can you point out where you live, on this map?

What do the squiggly red lines show? And why is one of them thicker?

Where are the highest mountains? Where's the flattest land?

What are the names of the seas around the islands?

Some islands are shown in a box. Why do you think that is?

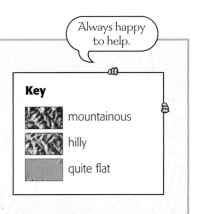

Key
- mountainous
- hilly
- quite flat

Your island home

In this unit you'll learn about the forces that shaped the British Isles – and about Britain's main physical features.

All change!

Your island home was not always an island. And not always here!

Once upon a time, around 380 million years ago, the British Isles lay at the equator, as part of a giant continent. When this broke up, they drifted north as part of Europe.

As they drifted, over millions of years, they went through many changes. They became desert. They were frozen in ice. They were drowned by the sea. They had earthquakes and eruptions. They got pushed and squeezed. And then they got cut off from the rest of Europe!

And here are the British Isles today, shaped by all those changes – and still changing.

And finally, our land is also being shaped and changed by humans! We haven't been here that long, but we've made a huge difference.

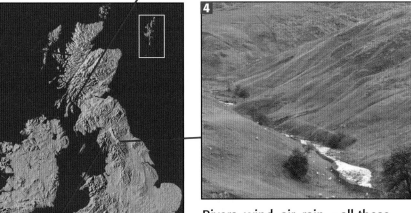

Rivers, wind, air, rain – all these helped to shape our land, and still do. This river is busy carving out its V-shaped valley.

The main cause of those changes was the powerful currents inside the Earth. These drag slabs of the Earth's crust around, causing earthquakes and eruptions, and pushing rock up into mountains.

Did you know?
- The currents inside the Earth are still at work.
- So 100 million years from now, the British Isles will be somewhere else!

Did you know?
- 500 million years ago, Scotland was not even joined to England.
- It lay on the floor of an ocean called Iapetus, far south of the Equator.

Ice also played a big part. In the Ice Ages, glaciers scoured out huge U-shaped valleys in Britain. You can still see them today.

The sea drowned us over and over, dumping sediment that formed new rock. It turned us into islands. And it's still busy shaping the coast.

X

Y

▲ *You'll find places like this in Britain …*

▲ *… and places like this.*

Your turn

1 This map shows the mountains that formed when rock got squeezed upwards, and some other features of the British Isles.

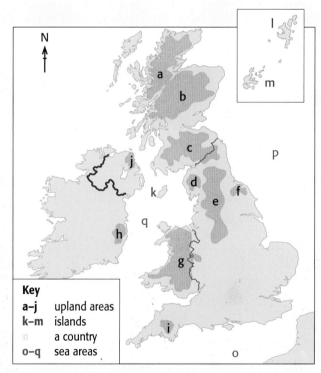

Key
a–j upland areas
k–m islands
n a country
o–q sea areas

a Your first task is to name all the places and features marked on the map. Page 127 will help.
Start your answer like this: *a =* _____
b Now explain why the islands marked **l** and **m** have been put in a box.

2 There are thousands of rivers in Britain, all busy shaping the land. See if you can identify these. (Page 127 will help.)
   A It's the longest river in Britain. It rises in Wales.
   B This one flows by the Houses of Parliament.
   C Stoke-on-Trent sits on this river.
   D Newcastle sits on this one.
   E This one runs along part of the border between England and Scotland.
   F Did Aberdeen get part of its name from this?
   G This one flows to the Wash, on the North Sea.

3 The photos above were taken at **A** and **B** on this little map.

   a Which photo was taken at which place? Explain your choice.
   b Both places were shaped by nature.
      i Which one also shows signs of being shaped by humans?
      ii What do you think it may have looked like, before humans arrived?
   c Write a paragraph comparing the two places. Say what's similar about them, and what's different.

4 You live on an island. Do you think that's a good thing? Make a list of the advantages of living on an island, and then list the disadvantages.

5 Finally, write a paragraph saying where on the Earth the British Isles is, at present. Include these terms:
equator   ocean   continent   Arctic Circle

It's a jigsaw!

In this unit you'll see how we humans have carved up the British Isles.

Building borders

8000 years ago there were no borders in these islands – because hardly anyone lived here.

But over time, different tribes arrived. They fought over things like land, trade and religion.

Eventually these borders were created between different areas. They still cause problems today!

That's just the start!

As the last map above shows, the British Isles is divided into two **countries**: the United Kingdom (UK) and the Republic of Ireland.

The United Kingdom in turn is made up of different **nations**: England, Scotland, Wales and Northern Ireland.

But that's just the start of the jigsaw. For example England and Scotland are divided into the **regions** shown this map.

Each region is in turn divided into smaller pieces. This makes it easier to manage services, such as education and health.

So who's in charge?

The UK is governed from London, its capital city. In Parliament, MPs vote on policies, and pass laws, that affect the whole UK.

Scotland also has a Parliament, in Edinburgh. It can pass laws on matters that affect only Scotland.

Wales has a National Assembly, based in Cardiff. Northern Ireland has one based in Belfast. These can't make laws. But they can make decisions about health services, education and other matters, for their own regions.

Remember!

the British Isles

the United Kingdom

Great Britain
(or just Britain)

Some facts about the British Isles

Area (square kilometres)	130 400	77 100	20 800	14 200	70 300
Population (millions)	50.5	5.1	3.0	1.7	4.2

Fact box

1801: Ireland becomes part of 'The United Kingdom of Great Britain and Ireland'.

1922: the Republic of Ireland gains independence.

1536: Henry VIII officially unites England and Wales.

1171: King Henry II of England takes control of Ireland.

1100: England, Scotland, Wales and Ireland are separate countries.

1603: King James VI of Scotland becomes King James I of England, giving the Union of the Crowns.

1276: King Edward I of England takes control of Wales.

1707: England, Scotland and Wales officially become Great Britain.

Today: England, Scotland, Wales and Northern Ireland are still united as the UK.

Your turn

1 The British Isles is divided like a jigsaw. Arthur lives in all these parts of the jigsaw:

British Isles
Great Britain
Scotland
Highlands and Islands
Fort William

DO NOT ENTER

Do the same to show where you live.
(But if you live in Fort William, do it for a person living in Land's End. See the map on page 127.)
You may need to ask your teacher for help.

2 Compare the map opposite with the one on page 127. In which region of Scotland is:
  a Dundee?   b Glasgow?
  c Aberdeen?   d Edinburgh?

3 In which region of England is:
  a Liverpool?   b Portsmouth?
  c Brighton?   d Bradford?
  e Ipswich?   f Newcastle-upon-tyne?

4 a Make a copy of this table. (Sketch the maps roughly. You can show the Shetlands in their correct place.)

	Great Britain	United Kingdom	British Isles
Population (millions)			
Area (____)			

  b Shade in the correct parts of each map.
  c Work out the population and area of the shaded parts, from the table at the top of the page.
  d Now give your table a suitable title.

5 Over the centuries, England fought many battles with Scotland, Ireland and Wales. Much blood was shed. The Fact box above shows just some key dates in this history. (No blood on show!)

Draw a timeline for the dates in the Fact box, from 1100 to today.
You could illustrate your timeline with small maps or flags or other symbols. Give it a suitable title.

What's our climate like?

In this unit you'll learn the difference between weather and climate – and how the climate varies across the UK.

Weather and climate

Weather means the state of the atmosphere. Is it warm? wet? windy? It changes from day to day.

Look at this weather map. With help from the key, you can tell that around **A** that day:

◆ it was quite cloudy and wet, but there was some sunshine.

◆ the temperature was around 6 °C.

◆ there was a south west wind (it blew *from* the south west).

◆ the wind was quite strong (around 38 miles per hour).

Climate is different from weather. It means what the weather is *usually* like. It is worked out by measuring the weather over many years, and then calculating the average.

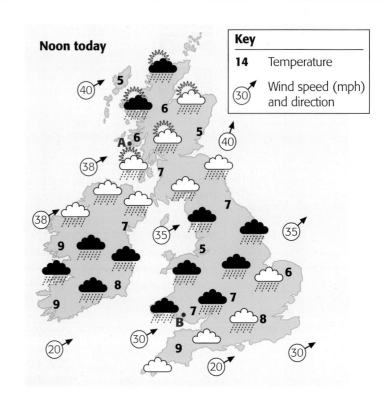

Noon today

Key	
14	Temperature
30	Wind speed (mph) and direction

Which parts are warmest? coldest?

Here are two climate maps. They show the *average* temperatures in summer and winter. The wavy lines are **isotherms**. Everywhere along an isotherm has the same average temperature. (*Iso-* means *the same*.)

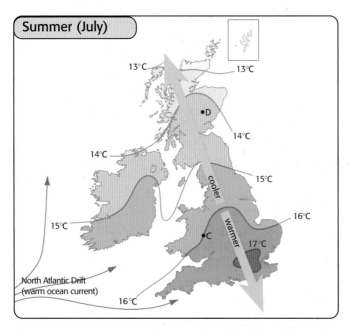

Summer (July)

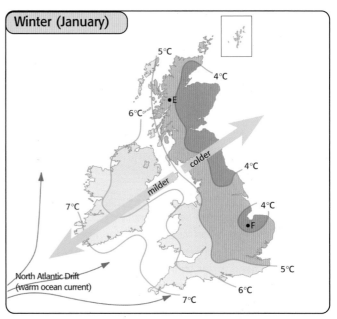

Winter (January)

As you can see, some places are cooler than others. In general:

◆ It is cooler in Scotland, because it is further from the equator.

◆ It is also cooler on high land. Up a mountain the temperature falls.

◆ But in winter, a warm ocean current called the **North Atlantic Drift** warms the west coast. So the east coast is the coldest part in winter.

Which parts are wettest?

On the right is another climate map. It shows the average rainfall in a year, for the British Isles. As you can see, some parts get a lot more rain than others.

Usually the higher parts are wetter. This is why:

Average annual rainfall

2 So the water vapour cools and condenses. Clouds form. It rains.

3 The rain falls on the **windward** side of the hill – facing the wind.

4 This side – the **leeward** side – stays quite dry.

1 High ground forces the warm, moist air to rise.

warm, moist air

5 The dry area on the leeward side is called the **rain shadow**.

prevailing wind direction

Key

average annual rainfall (mm)

mm
2400
1800
1200
800
600

Your turn

1 Look at the TV weather map on page 48.
  Find the place marked B.
  Describe what the weather was like in that area that day, as fully as you can.

2 Look at the first map at the bottom of page 48.
  a What is the temperature at C?
  b Which is the temperature at D?
   15 °C   14 °C   between 14 °C and 15 °C
  c Why is C warmer than D?

3 Now look at the second map.
  a What is the temperature at E?
  b What is the temperature at F?
  c Why is E warmer than F, even though it is further north?

4 Look at the rainfall map above.
  Four places are marked on it: A, B, C and D.
  a Which of them is wettest?
  b Which is driest?
  c One has an average rainfall of 2000 mm a year. Which one?
  d One has an annual rainfall of 500 mm a year. Which one?

5 Why do mountains help rain to form?

6 a What are *prevailing* winds?
  b The prevailing winds in the UK carry lots of moisture. Why? (Think about where they come from. The map on pages 128–129 will help.)

7 a Overall, which side of Great Britain is wettest? See if you can explain why. (Page 42?)
  b Now explain why B gets much less rain than C.

8 And now for a summary of what you've learned. On this map the British Isles is divided into four climate zones.
  a Make a larger, simpler, copy of the map.
  b Colour the land in each zone in a different colour.
  c Then add these four labels to their correct zones.

  warm summers, mild winters, not so wet

  mild summers, mild winters, wet

What's our weather usually like?

N

  warm summers, cold winters, dry

  mild summers, cold winters, not so wet

Where do we live?

In this unit you'll see how we humans have shaped the country, through where we chose to live!

Population density

About 64.5 million people live in the British Isles. About 60 million of us live in the UK. So are we all spread out evenly? The answer is No!

The **population density** of a place is the average number of people per square kilometre.

The map below shows how population density changes around the British Isles. The deep green regions are the least crowded. The deep red regions are the most crowded. As you can see, the population density varies a lot.

The UK's 10 largest cities

	Name	Population (millions)
1	London	7.17
2	Birmingham	0.98
3	Leeds	0.72
4	Glasgow	0.58
5	Sheffield	0.51
6	Bradford	0.47
7	Edinburgh	0.45
8	Liverpool	0.44
9	Manchester	0.39
10	Bristol	0.38

Did you know?
Of all the countries in the world, the UK ranks:
♦ 18th for size of population
♦ 45th for population density.

Did you know?
♦ London is the 26th largest city in the world.
♦ The largest one is Tokyo in Japan (population 26.8 million).

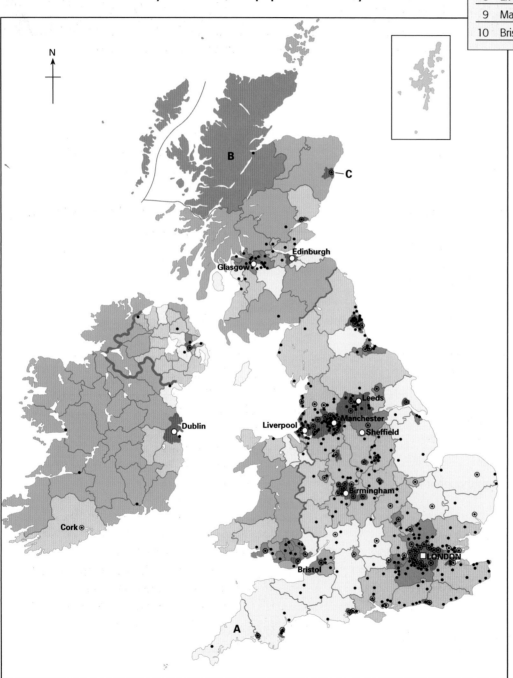

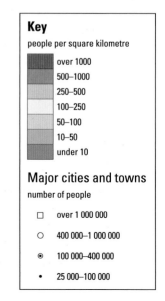

Key

people per square kilometre

▨	over 1000
▨	500–1000
▨	250–500
▨	100–250
▨	50–100
▨	10–50
▨	under 10

Major cities and towns

number of people

□	over 1 000 000
○	400 000–1 000 000
◉	100 000–400 000
•	25 000–100 000

▲ *Some places in the UK are quite empty, while some ...*

▲ *... are very crowded. What's your place like ?*

Your turn

1 Compare the two photos above.
   a Which place has the higher population density?
   b Which place is: **i** an urban area? **ii** a rural area? (Glossary?)

2 Look at the map on page 50. Some areas have been labelled with letters.
   a **i** What is the population density for area **A**? Give your answer in persons per square kilometre.
   ii Do you think *every* part of **A** has the same number of people per sq km? Explain.
   b **i** What is the population density for area **B**?
   ii See if you can explain why it's so low. (Page 42?)
   c Area **C** has a much higher population density than the area around it. Can you suggest a reason? (Page 54 has a clue.)
   d **i** Overall, where is the largest area of highest population density, in the British Isles?
   ii Suggest a reason why so many people live there. (Check out page 54?)
   e Do you think a map of population density would have looked the same 100 years ago? Explain.

3 The *average* population density for the UK is 248 people per sq km. Copy this table and see if you can fill in the names of the four nations (England, Wales, Scotland, Northern Ireland) in the correct places in the first column. The map on page 50 will help.

Nation	Average pop. density (persons/sq km)
	387
	66
	142
	121

4 Look again at the map on page 50. The main cities and towns are marked in. Can you see any link between the number of cities and towns in a region, and its population density? Explain.

5 Now look at this pie chart for the United Kingdom.

Where the UK population lives

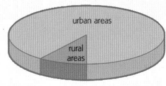

Is this statement true or false?
   a Most people in the UK live in the countryside.
   b Less than half of us live in towns and cities.
   c About 1/10 of the UK population lives in rural areas.

6 Next look at the list of UK top 10 cities on page 50.
   a Which two of the cities are in Scotland?
   b Where are the other eight?
   c Which is the largest city of all? How many times larger is it than: **i** Birmingham? **ii** Bristol?

7 Towns and cities can grow and spread until they join up, giving large built-up areas called **conurbations**. From the map on page 50, name 5 cities in *England* which are probably part of conurbations.

8 And finally, to round off this unit, write a report called *The pattern of population density around the UK*. Make it 100 – 150 words. Say clearly where the most crowded and least crowded regions are, and add other interesting details.

What kind of work do we do?

In this unit you'll find out what kinds of work people in the UK do for a living.

Different kinds of work

Economic activity is any work people get paid for.
(So homework does not count!)
You can divide it into four types or **sectors**:

Primary
Gathering materials from the Earth.
For example mining for coal, or growing wheat, or fishing.

Secondary or **manufacturing**
You turn materials into things to sell.
For example metal into car bodies or fish into fish nuggets.

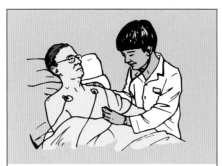

Tertiary or **service**
You provide a service for people.
Like teach them, or look after them when they're ill, or drive a taxi.

Quaternary
Hi-tech research. For example to develop a new medicine, or more advanced mobile phones.

▲ On the way to work, on a dark morning. (The truck drivers are working already.)

At work in the UK

Altogether, about 29 million people in the UK work for a living. (The total population is over 60 million.)

As this pie chart shows, most of them provide services.

The number in the quaternary sector is too small to show up!

What kind of work do we do, in the UK?

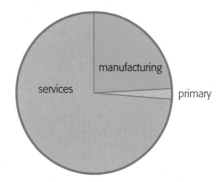

What is an industry?

Industry is just a general word for a branch of economic activity.
The car industry is made up of all the companies who make cars.

Economic activity in the UK

This map shows some of the UK's economic activity. Note that:

◆ farming goes on all around the UK. But there is only a little in the very hilly areas, where the farms are far apart. (Look back at the map on page 42.)

◆ lots of people in the UK earn a living from tourism.

◆ most industry is found around large towns and cities. It's one reason why they grew!

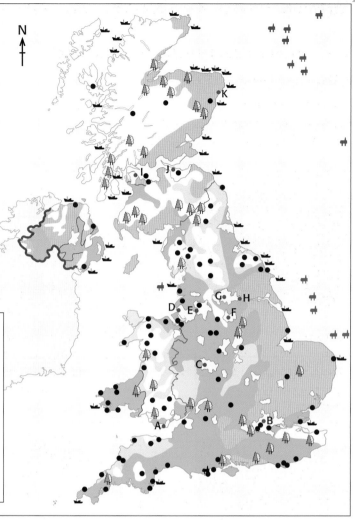

Key

☐	mostly hill farms (sheep)
▨	mostly livestock farms (animals for meat)
▨	mostly dairy farms (cattle for milk)
▨	mostly arable farms (crops)

🌲	forestry
⚓	fishing port
●	main tourism sites
◌	major industrial area
⚒	gas field
⚒	oil field
〰	international border
〰	national border

Your turn

1 What is *economic activity*?

2 Does this count as economic activity? Give a reason.
  a going to school   b doing a paper round
  c babysitting   d tidying your room

3 a Make a table with headings like this:

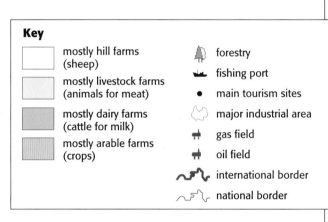

Primary	Secondary	Tertiary	Quaternary

  b Now write these jobs in the correct columns in your table:

  nurse   postman   boat builder
  oil rig worker actor   florist
  football star   fireman   farmer
  copper miner   architect   policeman
  bank manager   truck driver bee keeper
  gene researcher clergyman   inventor of robots

  c See if you can add *at least* ten other jobs to your table. Try for some for each sector. (Think about workers you see on TV, or on the way to school.)

4 Copy and complete, using words from the list below. (The pie chart on page 52 will help.)

  In the UK most people earn a living by providing _____. The _____ sector employs about _____ times as many people as _____ does, and about _____ times as many as the _____ _____.

  sector,   three,   primary,   tertiary,   manufacturing,   services,   forty

5 Look at Scotland on the map above. Give:
  a three primary activities off the coast
  b two primary activities on land

6 The map shows where tourism is important. Give six jobs connected with tourism. (Hint: tourists have to eat and sleep and travel.)

7 The map shows the main industrial areas, where you'll find factories. Compare these with the map of population density on page 50. What do you notice?

8 The red dots on the map above show 11 cities important for industry. (9 are in the 'top 10' list on page 50.) Name them. Start like this: A = _____ .

Richer? Poorer?

In this unit you'll learn that some parts of the UK are better off than others – and explore the reasons.

Fair pay?

This map shows how much workers earn a week, on average, in different regions. Why does it vary so much?

Key
Income, 2003

average weekly earnings

- over £475
- £425—£475
- £400—£425
- £375—£400
- £350—£375
- under £350
- no data

N

Earnings are high here because of the oil industry. The oil fields are in the North Sea.

100 years ago this area was wealthy – thanks to coal mining and other heavy industries. But most of them died away and the area grew poor. Now it is recovering.

This area was once wealthier because of coal. Now the mines are closed. (It's the same in Wales and other coal areas.)

This area has hardly any industry. But it has beautiful countryside and depends heavily on tourists.

Lots of new hi-tech companies are setting up in this area too.

This area never had many factories. The land is not so good for farming. There used to be tin mines but they have closed.

Earnings are high in this area because it has lots of hi-tech companies (making computers, software, mobile phones and so on).

London is the capital city, and a major centre of government, business, and tourism. Companies have head offices here. There are many highly paid jobs.

This has some of the UK's best farmland. It grows large amounts of crops.

▲ *You can tell a lot about how wealthy or poor an area is, just by looking.*

Your turn

1 This list gives weekly earnings for five people. Work out their *average* weekly earning. (Hint: add up and divide by 5.)

Brian	£400
Liz	£50
Anna	£500
Joe	£250
Richard	£1000

2 Look at the map on page 54.
   a What's the average weekly earning at **A**?
   b Does everyone in area **A** earn this much? Explain.
   c What's the average weekly earning at **B**?
   d Give reasons for the big difference in the figures for A and B.

3 Look at **C** on the map. Earnings in this area are higher than in the other areas around it. See if you can come up with a reason. (The map on page 53 may help.)

4 a Overall, where in the UK do people earn most?
   b Where do they earn least?
   Use terms like these in your answers: *south west, Wales, England, Scotland, north of* and so on.

5 So what helps to make an area wealthy?
   Show your answer as a spider map, like this one:

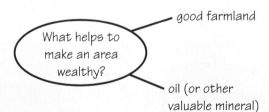

Page 54 will give you clues.

6 Now look at photos **A** and **B** at the top of the page.
   a Compare the two places. Which one seems to be poorer? What is your evidence?
   b What clues can you find that this place is poorer than it used to be?
   c What might have caused this change?

7 The government tries to help poorer areas.
   For example by:
   ◆ giving companies grants to set up new factories
   ◆ giving grants to improve roads and tourist facilities.
   This flow chart shows how a new factory can help a poorer area.

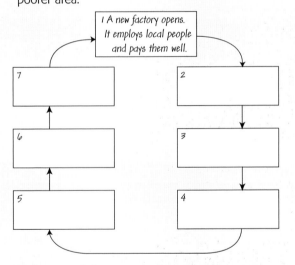

Make a much larger copy. (Use a whole page).
Then write these in the correct boxes:

   So the local people have more money to spend.

   So the shops get better, and other services (like restaurants and sports centres) open.

   So they buy more clothes and shoes and other goods.

   ... so more companies think about moving there.

   So the area becomes more attractive to live and work in ...

   So the local shops make more money.

8 Now do your own flow chart, to show how a new tourist attraction (for example a new nature park, or an exciting new museum) could help a poor area.

Scotland's National Parks

Here you'll find out about Scotland's National Parks: where they are, what they are like, why they were set up, and who runs them.

What is a National Park?

A National Park is a large area of land that is protected by law, so that it can be enjoyed by everyone.

There are National Parks all over the world. Some are in deserts and rainforests. There are 15 in Great Britain. And of these, 2 are in Scotland.

Places are turned into National Parks because they are special in some way, and need protection. They may have superb scenery, or a unique climate, or rare plants and animals. Between them, the two Scottish National Parks have all of those.

Loch Lomond & The Trossachs National Park

This was Scotland's first National Park, set up in 2002. It has some of Scotland's most stunning scenery.

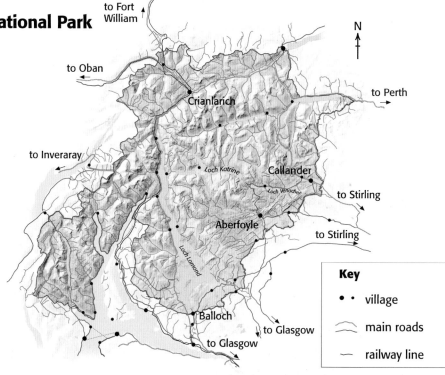

Key

- •• village
- ⌒ main roads
- — railway line

It has 20 Munros (mountains over 914 m, or 3000 feet) to thrill climbers. This is Ben More, the highest one.

It has dozens of lochs and lochans, of which Loch Lomond is the largest. And around 50 rivers and burns.

There are around 20 villages in the park. Around 15 600 people live in it. But most of it is quite empty.

Who manages them?

- ◆ Each is managed by its own National Park Authority.
- ◆ Some members of this body are chosen by the Scottish Executive and the local authorities.
- ◆ The rest live in the park, and are chosen by the park residents.

Who owns the National Parks?

The land has a mixture of owners:

- ◆ private owners (such as farmers)
- ◆ public bodies (the Forestry Commission and Scottish Water)
- ◆ Scotland's Woodland Trust, National Trust, and other charities

The Cairngorms National Park

This brilliant park was set up in 2003. It is twice as large as Loch Lomond and the Trossachs. It has 4 of Scotland's 5 highest mountains.

Above 600 m it's a wilderness. The ecosystem here is Alpine tundra, with its own special plants and animals.

So what can you do in the National Parks?

You can do an amazing range of things. For example you can:

◆ walk, climb, and, in winter in the Cairngorms, ski and snowboard.

◆ sail, canoe, kayak, windsurf, and fish.

◆ cycle, go quad-biking, or pony trekking, or dog-sledding in winter.

◆ watch wildlife. You may see a golden eagle. Red deer. Red squirrels. Or even reindeer in the Cairngorms.

If all that sounds too much, you can relax and do nothing, but breathe in Scotland's cleanest freshest air.

16 000 people live here, mostly in the towns. Many work in tourism. Farming is important too, especially for beef.

Your turn

1 a What is a National Park?
   b Who owns Scotland's National Parks?
   c Do you think a National Park is a good idea? Explain.

2 Look at the maps here and on page 127. Which park do you think gets more visitors? Explain your answer.

3 The UK has an average population density of 248 people per sq km.
   a Using data from this unit, calculate the population density for each of Scotland's two National Parks.
   b i Are the values greater or less than that for the UK?
     ii Which National Park is more 'empty'?
     Give reasons for each answer in b.

4 Now see if you can explain why:
   a most people in the Cairngorms work in tourism
   b an area like the Trossachs might need protection.
   Come up with as many reasons as you can.

5 Below are the aims of the National Park Authorities. For each aim, see if you can think up *two* examples of how they could meet that aim. (Glossary?)

   The National Park Authority
   Its aims are to …
   ◆ protect the beauty, wildlife and traditions of the Park
   ◆ help visitors to enjoy the Park
   ◆ promote the economic and social well-being of the people who live in it.

Weather

The big picture

This chapter is all about **weather**. These are the big ideas behind the chapter:

- Weather is the state of the atmosphere around us at any given time. (Warm? wet? windy?) It can change from day to day.
- Different aspects of the weather can be measured.
- Rain always depends on moist air rising, and cooling.
- Air rising and falling means changes in air pressure, and that means wind.
- Extreme rain, wind and storms can kill, and do a huge amount of damage.

Your goals for this chapter

By the end of this chapter you should be able to answer these questions:

- What does this weather term mean?

    temperature   precipitation   air pressure   wind speed
    wind direction   cloud cover   visibility

- How is each item above measured – and what units are used?
- What are the three different kinds of rainfall, and how does each form?
- What kind of weather is linked with:

    low pressure?   high pressure in summer?   high pressure in winter?

- Why can the weather in the UK change very quickly?
- What are these, and how would you show them on a weather map?

    warm front   cold front

- What is the monsoon season, and why and where does it occur?
- Why does Bangladesh have such severe flooding?
- What is a hurricane, and how does one form?
- Why are hurricanes able to do so much damage?

And then …

When you finish the chapter, come back to this page and see if you have met your goals!

Did you know?
- The wettest place in the world is Cherrapunji in India.
- It gets about 12.7 metres of rain/year – most of it in the monsoon season.

Did you know?
- Weather exists only in the lowest 10 km of the atmosphere.

Did you know?
- During the last Ice Age a third of the Earth was covered in ice – over 240 m thick.
- It ended around 12 500 years ago. (Lucky us!)

Did you know?
- The lowest ever recorded temperature was −89.2 °C, in Antarctica, on 21 July 1983.

Your chapter starter

Look at the photo on page 58.

What's the white stuff?

What caused it?

How would it feel to be there? What kinds of things could you do?

What might this place look like in six months' time?

Out, penguin.

Measuring and mapping the weather

In this unit you will find out how the weather is measured – and how to read simple weather maps.

Measuring the weather

Weather is the state of the atmosphere at a given time. You can tell a lot about it just by looking.

But to describe it fully, you need to ask questions like these. And answer them by measuring!

All around the world, night and day, the weather is continually monitored and measured. At weather stations on land, and by special equipment on planes, ships, weather balloons, and in satellites.

Then **meteorologists** or weather scientists use the data to write weather reports, and draw weather maps, and make weather forecasts.

Your turn

1 First, look at the weather map on the right. It's the kind of map you see on TV and in the newspapers.
   Below are symbols it uses. Say what you think each means:

   a   b

   c   d

   e   f   27

   g   20   h   **16**

2 The photo above shows Seaburn on the day this weather map was drawn. Find it on the weather map.
   What can you say about the weather around there?
   Describe it as fully as you can, giving some figures.

3 Now say what you think the weather was like at:
   a **X** on the weather map   b **Y** on the weather map

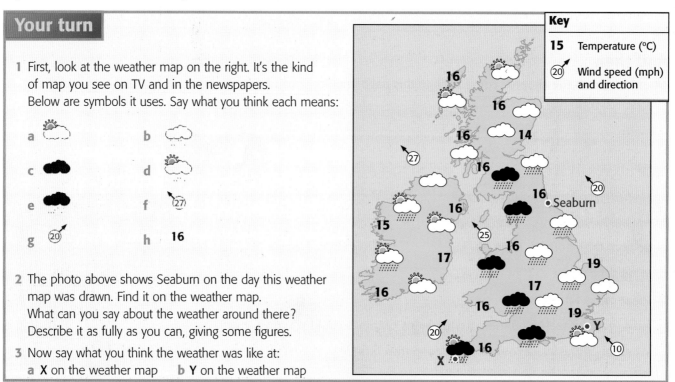

Key

15	Temperature (°C)
20	Wind speed (mph) and direction

Weather term	Means ...	Usually given ...	Measured using ...
temperature	exactly how hot or cold it is		
	how 'heavy' the air is	in millibars (mb)	
	how much of the sky is hidden by clouds		your eyes; satellite image
	how fast the wind is blowing		
	where the wind is blowing from (a south west wind blows from the south west)	as a compass bearing (N, NW, SW and so on)	
	water falling from the sky in any form (rain, hail, sleet, snow)		
	how far ahead we can see, for example on a foggy day	in metres or kilometres	

4 This question is all about measuring the weather.
You have to work out the answers for yourself, just like
a detective. (The glossary will help.)

a First, make a copy of the table above.

b Write the words from list **A** below in the first column
of your table, in the correct places.

c Complete the third column using list **B**.
Start with the easiest units.

A Weather terms	**B** Units
wind direction	kilometres or miles
visibility	per hour (like a car)
air pressure	millilitres
precipitation	oktas
wind speed	degrees Centigrade (°C)
cloud cover	

5 Now look at box **C**. It shows equipment for measuring
the weather. Look at each item in turn. What do you
think it measures? Write its name in the correct place
in the fourth column of your table.

6 **Cloud cover** means how much of the sky is covered in
cloud. It is one thing you can measure just by looking.
Cloud cover is measured in eighths or oktas, like this:

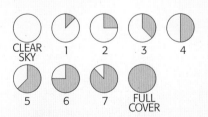

CLEAR SKY   1   2   3   4

5   6   7   FULL COVER

Note!
They use more
complex symbols
for oktas on
weather charts.

a Now look at the photo on page 60. As far as one can
tell from a photo, what do you think the cloud cover
was at Seaburn that day? Answer in oktas.

b Do the same for the photo on page 58.

7 a Look back at your table. Which of those aspects of
the weather could you measure at home?

b Choose one. Say **how** you would measure it, and
when. Draw a diagram to show any equipment
you'd use, and where you would place it.

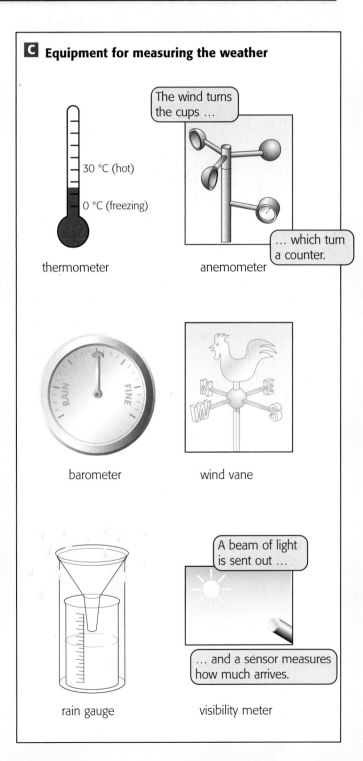

C **Equipment for measuring the weather**

The wind turns the cups ...

30 °C (hot)

0 °C (freezing)

thermometer   anemometer

... which turn a counter.

RAIN   FINE

barometer   wind vane

A beam of light is sent out ...

... and a sensor measures how much arrives.

rain gauge   visibility meter

So it's raining ...

In this unit you will be reminded about the water cyle, and learn about three different types of rainfall.

The water cycle

It is pouring with rain. You are soaking. Your hair is dripping. Your socks are soggy. So where is all this water coming from? It's the **water cycle** at work! Follow the numbers to see how:

3 When air rises, it cools. So the water vapour in it **condenses** into tiny water droplets. These form clouds.

4 Clouds get carried along by the wind. The droplets inside them grow into larger drops, leading to ...

5 ... **precipitation**. The water drops fall as rain (or hail or sleet or snow). Get your raincoat on!

2 The water vapour mixes with the air. We can't see it, but it's there! It can travel far from the ocean.

6 Some water runs along the ground, and some soaks through it, heading for streams and rivers.

7 The river carries the water back to the ocean. The cycle is complete. And then it starts all over again ...

1 The sun warms oceans, lakes and seas, turning water into water vapour, a gas. This is called **evaporation**.

Evaporation goes on non-stop, from the oceans, lakes, and seas. And the water vapour travels easily, since it is a gas. So there is always some water vapour in the air, even hundreds of miles from water.

Those rain essentials

So, just two things are needed, to give rain:

◆ the air must contain enough water vapour, and

◆ the air must rise and cool, so that the water vapour condenses.

Three types of rainfall

All rain is just water. All rain is caused by air rising. But it can rise for different reasons – so we give the rainfall different names.

Convectional rainfall

Here the air rises because the ground heats it. It rises in warm currents. We call these **convection currents**. So we call the rain **convectional rainfall**.

In the UK we get convectional rainfall inland in summer, where the ground gets hottest, far from the cooling effects of the sea.

3 The rising air cools. The water vapour condenses. Clouds form. It rains.

2 Currents of warm air rise.

1 The sun warms the ground … which then warms the air above it.

Relief rainfall

Wind is moving air.

When the wind meets a line of high hills or mountains, there's only one way to go – up ! So the air rises and cools – and we get rain. We call it **relief rainfall**.

In the UK the prevailing wind is from the south west. So we get relief rainfall on the high land along the west coast.

3 The rising air cools. The water vapour condenses. Clouds form. It rains.

2 The air is forced to rise.

1 Warm moist air arrives from the Atlantic Ocean.

leeward (sheltered)

4 The rain falls on the **windward** side of the mountain. The **leeward** side stays dry.

windward (facing the wind)

Frontal rainfall

As you'll see in Unit 5.4, huge blocks of air called **air masses** move around the Earth.

When a warm air mass meets a cold one, the warm air is forced to rise. So we get rain. This is **frontal rainfall**.

We can get this type of rainfall anywhere, since air masses can travel anywhere. But in the UK, they often arrive in from the Atlantic Ocean. So the west of the UK gets a lot of frontal rainfall.

warm

2 The warm air mass slides up over the cold one, or gets driven up by it.

3 The rising air cools. The water vapour condenses. Clouds form. It rains.

1 A warm air mass meets a cold air mass.

cold

Your turn

1 To form clouds, two things are always needed. Which are they? Choose from this list:
   wind   rising air   mountains   hot sun
   warm ground   water vapour

2 a Do you think clouds can form in the dark? Explain.
   b Can there be rain without clouds? Explain.

3 Which type of rainfall is the result of:
   a mountains in the way?
   b a mass of warm air meeting a mass of cold air?

4 Now see if you can explain why the west coast of Scotland gets a lot of rain, and name the two main types of rainfall there.

Air pressure and weather

Here you'll learn about the weather you get with high and low air pressure.

What's air pressure?

Although we can't feel it, all the air above us is pressing down on us, giving **air pressure**. If air pressure is **low**, it means air is rising. If it is **high** it means air is sinking. And each brings different weather.

▲ *Low pressure weather !*

Low pressure weather

Look what happens when warm air rises …

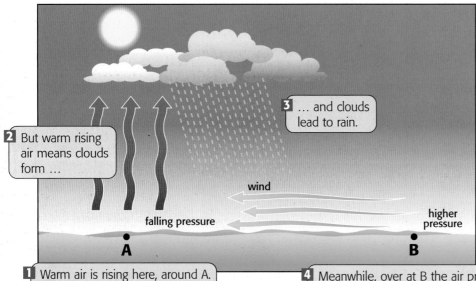

2 But warm rising air means clouds form …

3 … and clouds lead to rain.

wind

falling pressure

higher pressure

A

B

1 Warm air is rising here, around A. So the air pressure falls at A.

4 Meanwhile, over at B the air pressure is higher. So air rushes from B to A as **wind**.

So a fall in air pressure is a sign of rain and wind.
The lower the pressure the worse the weather will be.

High pressure weather

When warm air rises in one place, cool air sinks somewhere else.

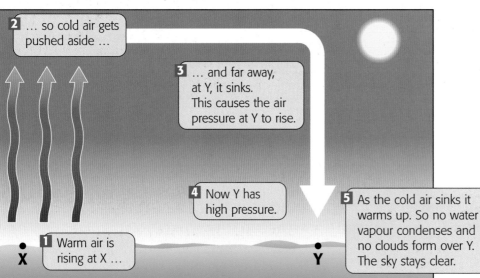

2 … so cold air gets pushed aside …

3 … and far away, at Y, it sinks. This causes the air pressure at Y to rise.

1 Warm air is rising at X …

4 Now Y has high pressure.

5 As the cold air sinks it warms up. So no water vapour condenses and no clouds form over Y. The sky stays clear.

X

Y

So high pressure means no clouds. Which means it gives us our hottest summer weather and coldest winter weather, as you'll see next.

▲ *To see if the air pressure is rising or falling, check a barometer.*

When there's high pressure in summer …

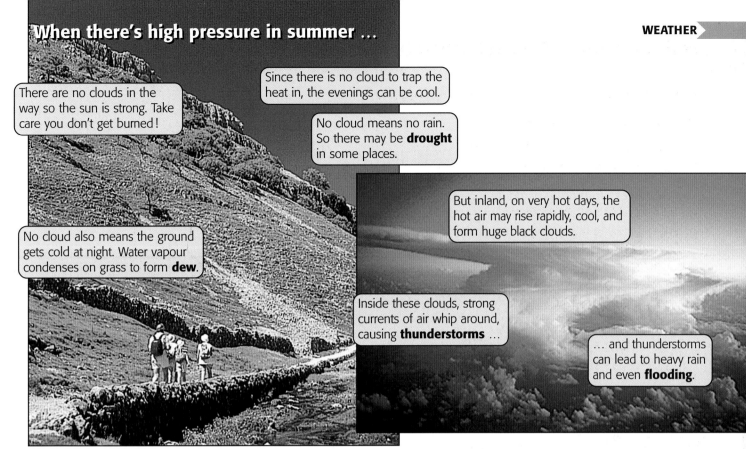

There are no clouds in the way so the sun is strong. Take care you don't get burned!

Since there is no cloud to trap the heat in, the evenings can be cool.

No cloud means no rain. So there may be **drought** in some places.

No cloud also means the ground gets cold at night. Water vapour condenses on grass to form **dew**.

But inland, on very hot days, the hot air may rise rapidly, cool, and form huge black clouds.

Inside these clouds, strong currents of air whip around, causing **thunderstorms** …

… and thunderstorms can lead to heavy rain and even **flooding**.

When there's high pressure in winter …

There is no cloud to act as a blanket. So the days are clear, cold and bright.

With no cloud, the ground cools fast at night and cools the air above it. Water vapour condenses and freezes on cold surfaces, giving **frost**.

It also condenses on dust and other particles in the air, giving **fog**. This makes driving dangerous.

Pipes may burst and homes may get flooded.

Water on roads freezes into ice as the sun goes down.

Ice and frost mean animals have trouble finding food.

Your turn

1 Write this out, using the correct word from each pair.

Low pressure is a sign of fine/unsettled weather. The lower the pressure the calmer/stormier the weather will be. High pressure brings clear/cloudy skies, which means very hot/cold weather in summer and very warm/cold weather in winter.

2 For some jobs, long spells of high pressure weather can bring problems. Try to give three examples.

3 For some jobs, long spells of low pressure weather can bring problems. Write down three examples.

4 It's August, and high pressure. You're going camping. List four items you'll pack, to cope with the weather.

5 a What do fog, dew and frost have in common?
b Explain how each forms.

6 Which type of weather do you prefer – high or low pressure? And in which season? Give your reasons.

Sudden changes in our weather

In this unit you will learn why our weather in the UK can change so quickly.

Air masses

Some parts of the world are hot. Some are cold. The result is that the air moves around – like the air in a cold room when you turn on a heater.

The air moves around the world in huge blocks called **air masses**. An air mass can be thousands of km across. It can be warm or cold, damp or dry, depending on where it came from.

An air mass coming from the North Pole will be cold and dry …

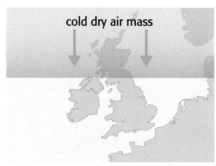

… so if it moves over the UK you'll get cold dry weather.

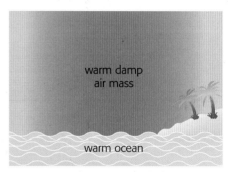

An air mass coming from a warm ocean will be warm and damp …

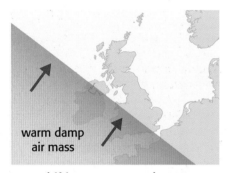

… and if it moves over the UK you get warm dampish weather.

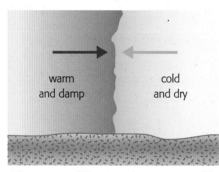

Often, two different air masses will meet and clash over the UK …

… and the result is sudden changes in the weather!

Many different air masses cross Britain. That's why our weather can change so fast. But when an air mass moves very slowly, or sits still for a while, we get the same weather for days.

Fronts

The leading edge of an air mass is called a **front**.

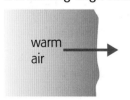

A **warm front** means a warm air mass is arriving.

That is shown on a weather map by red frills.

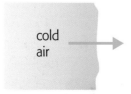

A **cold front** means a cold air mass is arriving.

That is shown on a weather map by blue spikes.

the cold front has caught up with the warm one here

Here a cold front is chasing a warm one. (We call this a **depression**.)

When a new front reaches the UK, it always brings a change in the weather.

When a warm front arrives

8 am

It's cool and dry. The sky is clear.

midday

warm front

warm air sliding up

4 pm

Time to put away the brolly!

There's a cold air mass over your area. But a warm front is on the way.

How will it affect the weather?

1 Warm air is lighter. So it slides up over the cold air.
2 As it rises, the pressure falls. So the weather gets a bit windy.
3 The rising air cools. The water vapour condenses to form a sloping bank of cloud.
4 It starts to rain. It may rain for hours.

Now the front has passed. The warm air mass has taken over.

So the temperature has risen. The rain has eased off. The wind has dropped.

When a cold front arrives

8 am

Nice and warm – but a bit cloudy!

midday

cold front

cold air pushing under

1 pm

I wish I'd brought my coat!

There's a warm air mass over your area. But a cold front is on the way.

How will it affect the weather?

1 The heavy cold air advances fast. It pushes sharply under the warm air.
2 So the pressure rises sharply, causing strong gusty winds.
3 As the warm air is driven upwards, its water vapour condenses. A steep bank of thick cloud forms.
4 It rains heavily. You may even get thunderstorms.

Now the front has passed. (Cold fronts travel much faster than warm ones!)

The cold air mass has taken over. So it is cooler. The rain has stopped. The sky is clearing.

Your turn

1 What is an air mass?

2 Five main types of air mass cross Britain. This map shows where they come from. (See page 129 too.) Answer these questions using the labels A – E:
   a Which air mass is coldest, and dry? Why?
   b Which two are dampest? Why?
   c Which one is very cold and dry in winter, but warmer in summer? Try to explain why.
   d Which one is warm even in winter?

3 What is: a a warm front?   b a cold front? Draw symbols for them. Beside each symbol write *warmer* and *colder* where you think they should go.

4 It is 7 am on 16 March. There is a cold air mass in your area. A warm front will arrive about 4 pm. Write a weather forecast for your local radio.

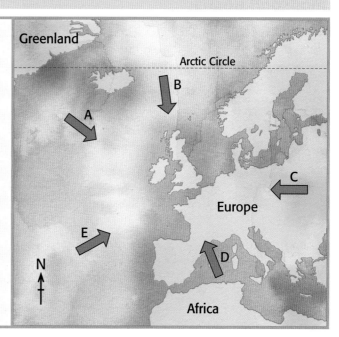

Monsoon: too much rain?

In this unit you will find out what the monsoon rains are – and about the floods they cause in Bangladesh.

The monsoon rains

Some parts of the UK get quite a lot of rain. But think about Bangladesh. On average, it gets nearly three times as much rain a year as the UK – and most of it falls between May and September. This part of the year is called the **monsoon season**. The rains are the **monsoon rains**.

What causes the monsoon rains?

As the map above shows, the monsoon rains fall over a large part of south Asia, not just Bangladesh. This is what causes them:

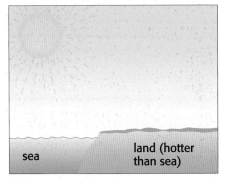

Land heats up faster than the ocean, in summer. So, by May, the land in south Asia is a lot hotter than the ocean around it.

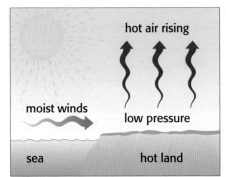

The land heats the air. The hot air rises fast, giving low pressure. So moist winds blow in from the ocean to fill the pressure 'gap'.

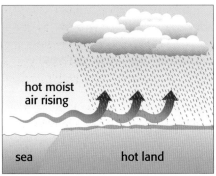

The moist air in the winds rises over the hot land, leading to clouds, and torrential rain – and more wind!

By September the land is cooling. The ocean is cooling too, but more slowly. (Land cools more slowly than water.) So now the wind changes direction. It blows from the land to the ocean – so the rainfall decreases.

Monsoon floods

The monsoon rains bring some severe flooding to south Asia. Bangladesh suffers worst of all. (You will see why in the next unit.)

▲ Monsoon floods in the streets of Dhaka, the capital of Bangladesh.

◄ This family has rescued what it could, by raft, from its flooded home.

Floods in Bangladesh, 2004

Bangladesh suffers heavy moonsoon flooding every year. In 2004, the floods were even worse than usual.

Death toll reaches 500 as floods cover Bangladesh

The death toll for this year's floods in Bangladesh has now reached 500. After three weeks of the worst flooding in 15 years, over two-thirds of the country is under water.

Heavy monsoon rains in Bangladesh and its neighbours have caused the country's three big rivers to flood at the same time.

In Dhaka, thousands of people waded through dirty water, looking for safety in a high-rise building, or a school, or a flood shelter. 'This is bad' said Fatima Begum, as she struggled to carry her two children. 'The floods got into the sewage system and now there's sewage everywhere. It has polluted the water supply so we've no clean water. I am so worried my childen will fall ill.'

Water is one problem. Food is another – it is getting harder and harder to find. And the live cables that dangle everywhere add extra danger.

Out in the countryside, all is misery. Reeza Lal and his family huddle under an old plastic sheet on a muddy embankment. Below them, in the swirling river, the swollen bodies of dead cows and chickens bob along in the water, along with tin bowls, and roof beams, and broken furniture.

'I don't know what to do,' said Reeza. 'We have no food, or water. We don't know when we can go home again. My crops have been washed away. My animals have drowned. We have lost everything.'

From newspaper reports, 30 July 2004

Flood factfile, Bangladesh 2004

Duration: 1 month
Final death toll: over 1000 people
Homeless: over 7 million people
Destroyed or badly damaged:
2.6 million homes
11 000 schools
3000 bridges
30 000 km of roads
2 million hectares of crops
Cost of damage: £4 billion

▲ *It's her job to look after her little brother, and keep him safe.*

Your turn

1 You have to explain in simple words, to an 8-year-old, why monsoon rains occur. What will you say?

2 Where is Bangladesh? Which country surrounds it? (Check out the map on page 129 too.)

3 The bar graph on the right shows rainfall in Dhaka in Bangladesh, through the year.
   a Which month gets most rain? Can you explain why?
   b Why does November get much less rain than June?
   c About how much rain does Dhaka get in a year?
      About: **i** 340 mm **ii** 170 cm **iii** 1700 cm

4 Imagine you are the boy in the red T-shirt, in the photo on page 68. Write a diary entry about your day.

5 Now imagine you are the boy's mother, behind him in the photo. You are feeling really worried. Tell us why.

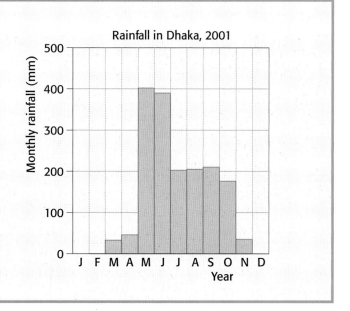

Rainfall in Dhaka, 2001

Monthly rainfall (mm)

Year

A closer look at flooding in Bangladesh

Here you'll find out why Bangladesh has such severe flooding, and how it copes.

Why does Bangladesh have such severe floods?

Bangladesh suffers heavy flooding every year. This shows why:

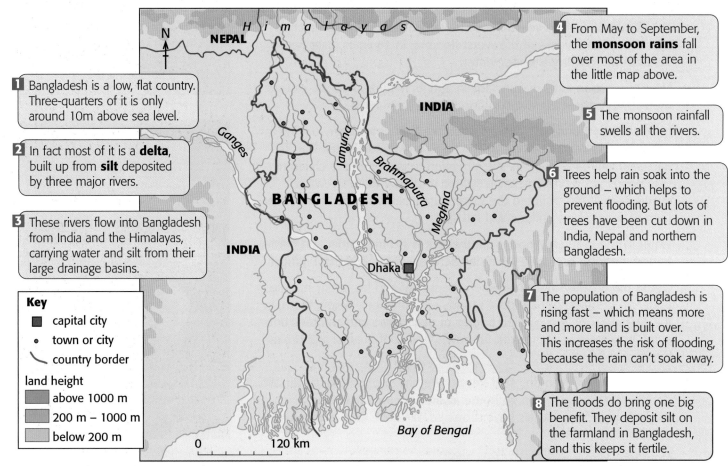

1 Bangladesh is a low, flat country. Three-quarters of it is only around 10m above sea level.

2 In fact most of it is a **delta**, built up from **silt** deposited by three major rivers.

3 These rivers flow into Bangladesh from India and the Himalayas, carrying water and silt from their large drainage basins.

4 From May to September, the **monsoon rains** fall over most of the area in the little map above.

5 The monsoon rainfall swells all the rivers.

6 Trees help rain soak into the ground – which helps to prevent flooding. But lots of trees have been cut down in India, Nepal and northern Bangladesh.

7 The population of Bangladesh is rising fast – which means more and more land is built over. This increases the risk of flooding, because the rain can't soak away.

8 The floods do bring one big benefit. They deposit silt on the farmland in Bangladesh, and this keeps it fertile.

Key
- ■ capital city
- • town or city
- ⌐ country border

land height
- ▨ above 1000 m
- ▨ 200 m – 1000 m
- ▨ below 200 m

0   120 km

So climate and **relief** (the height of the land) play a big part in the flooding. But human actions make it worse. At least one third of Bangladesh is flooded every year.

Comparing the UK and Bangladesh

The UK is more **developed** than most countries. That means people have a good standard of living, overall.

It has a good **infrastructure** (roads, phone system, water supply, electricity supply and so on). And most people have enough money to live on.

Bangladesh is less developed, as you can see from this table. The infrastructure is poor. 90% of the roads are not paved – they are just dirt tracks. Many people live in great poverty.

Severe flooding will be a big problem for any country, even a rich one like the UK. But for a poor country like Bangladesh, the problem is massive.

Comparing the UK and Bangladesh		
	UK	**Bangladesh**
Population (millions)	59	136
Area (sq km)	243 000	144 000
Number of people/ per sq km	244	1042
Average amount people earn a year	£18 600	£124
The % of people living in rural areas	10%	84%
Length of paved roads per 1000 sq km of land	1531 km	138 km
Number of phone lines per 1000 people	587	4
Number of radios per 1000 people	1406	45
Number of TVs per 1000 people	508	6

How does Bangladesh cope with flooding?

Bangladesh makes huge efforts to cope with flooding. But it's a struggle.

Many buildings – like this house – are built on stilts to protect them from floods.

Hundreds of km of **embankments** have been built along rivers, to keep the water in – but not everywhere.

There are warnings when floods are on the way – but it is hard to warn the people in rural areas.

When floods arrive, the police and army do what they can – but they can't be everywhere.

Some flood shelters are built – but not nearly enough. People shelter wherever they can.

After bad floods they need help from the rest of the world: food, tents, seeds, medicine, money.

Your turn

1 Bangladesh is a *delta*. Explain that term. (Glossary?)

2 Bangladesh has a huge flood problem. See if you can explain the part each of these plays:
   a It is in the drainage basin of three major rivers.
   b It is low and flat.
   c Rain is not spread evenly through the year. Most falls in a 5-month period.
   d The population almost doubled between 1975 and 2005.
   e 2 billion tonnes of silt are carried into Bangladesh each year, and most is deposited on the river beds.

3 Bangladesh has a far higher risk of flooding than the UK does. Give at least three reasons to explain why.

4 Above are ways Bangladesh responds to flooding. Using the glossary to help you, decide which ones are:
   a short-term b long term

5 Using the data in the table on page 70, explain why:
   a it's hard to warn people that floods are on the way, in Bangladesh.
   b it's hard to get help to the flood victims.

6 *Bangladesh should build embankments along all its rivers*. Do you think this is a good idea? Explain fully.

7 *Flooding helps to keep Bangladesh poor*. Do you think tthat could be true? Give your reasons.

8 *The richer and more developed a country is, the better it can cope with floods*. Do you agree? Explain.

Hurricane!

In this unit you will learn about hurricanes: what they are, how they form, and the damage they can do.

What is a hurricane?

A hurricane is a huge storm system that starts over warm tropical ocean waters. It spins as it moves. If it reaches land, it can do terrible damage. This is how a hurricane forms:

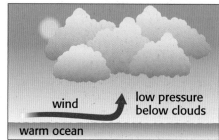

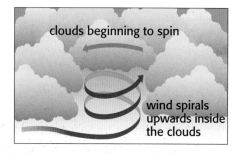

Warm moist air rises fast from the ocean surface. As it rises its water vapour condenses, forming clouds. The clouds can quickly grow into tall heavy thunderclouds ...

... like these. Below the thunderclouds, the warm moist air is still rising fast, leaving low pressure on the ocean surface. So wind rushes in, and up.

Because of the Earth's rotation, the wind does not go straight up. It spirals, making the clouds spin. (They always spin anti-clockwise in the northern hemisphere.)

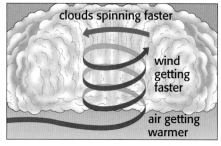

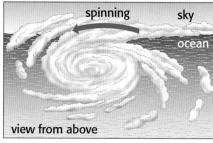

When water vapour condenses, it gives out heat. This makes the air even warmer. The clouds rise and expand. The pressure drops further. The wind rushes in even faster.

And so the system grows and spreads. It is now a **tropical storm**, with winds over 100 km an hour. As it spins, the clouds cluster tighter. Soon it looks like ...

...a big wheel of cloud with a small hole in the middle. It keeps growing, and spinning faster, fed by the warm damp air from below. Once the wind speed reaches ...

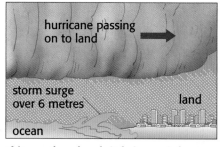

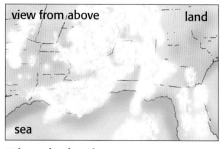

... an average of 119 km an hour, it's called a **hurricane**. Wind speed can reach over 250 km an hour. And the whole hurricane can move forward at over 30 km an hour.

If it reaches land, it brings violent winds, torrential rain, and **storm surges** of sea water. These surges occur because the low pressure draws the sea water upwards.

When the hurricane moves over cool ocean water, or onto dry land, it starts to die away – because now there is no warm moist air to feed it.

A satellite image of a hurricane

This photo shows a hurricane in the Gulf of Mexico, heading for the coast of the USA. It was taken by a satellite.

over 600 km

The hole at the very centre is called the **eye** of the hurricane. You can see the ocean through it.

Inside the eye, all is calm. No clouds, little wind. (The wind spirals up the walls of the eye.)

The dense wall of cloud around the eye is called the **eye wall**. This is where the wind is fiercest.

The bands of cloud that spiral out from the eye wall are called **rain bands**. Guess why!

Different oceans, different names

A hurricane can start in any warm tropical ocean water. But it has different names in different oceans, as this map shows.

Each hurricane is given a person's name, to stop people getting them mixed up. The names are chosen in advance: girl, boy, girl, boy. For example Ana, Bill, Claudette, Danny, …

The hurricane shown above was called Katrina. It occurred in 2005. You can find out more about it in the next unit.

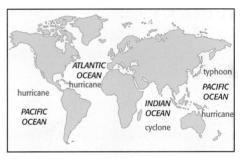

▲ Other names for hurricanes.

The hurricane scale

The stronger a hurricane, the more damage it can do.

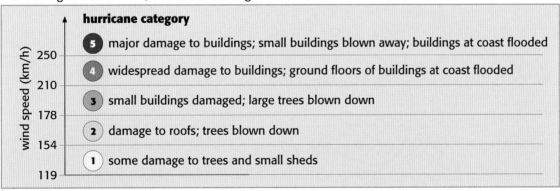

hurricane category

wind speed (km/h)

- **5** major damage to buildings; small buildings blown away; buildings at coast flooded
- **4** widespread damage to buildings; ground floors of buildings at coast flooded
- **3** small buildings damaged; large trees blown down
- **2** damage to roofs; trees blown down
- **1** some damage to trees and small sheds

250
210
178
154
119

Your turn

1 Explain what this term means, *in your own words*:
   a hurricane   b the eye of a hurricane
   c a storm surge   d a category 5 hurricane

2 A challenge. See if you can write a summary of how hurricanes form – in not more than 6 bullet points!

3 Give two ways in which hurricanes can cause flooding.

4 See if you can explain why hurricanes won't form:
   a if the ocean surface water is cool
   b if there are already strong winds in the area
   c off the west coast of Scotland

Hurricane Katrina

Here you will follow a hurricane on its journey, and see what damage it can do. We take hurricane Katrina as example.

Katrina on the way

On August 23, 2005, hurricane Katrina was born in the North Atlantic Ocean, as a tropical storm. It made its way onto land, in North America. It lived for 8 days, in different forms before, it died away. But in that time:

- it travelled over 4500 km, from birth to final death as a depression
- it caused over 1800 deaths
- it left hundreds of thousands of people homeless, and jobless
- it devastated towns and cities
- it did over 100 billion dollars' worth of damage. (The final count could be 150 billion.)

▲ *A street in New Orleans on 29 August, after Katrina had passed.*

Katrina's route

This shows Katrina's route:

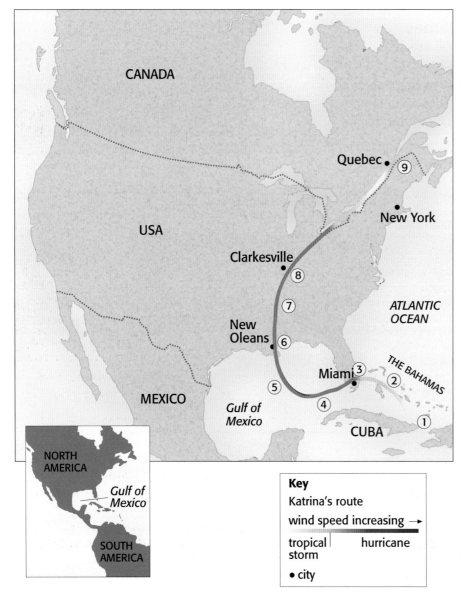

CANADA

Quebec ⑨

New York

USA

Clarkesville
⑧

⑦

New
Oleans ⑥

ATLANTIC
OCEAN

Miami ③

THE BAHAMAS

②

⑤

MEXICO

Gulf of
Mexico

④

①

CUBA

NORTH
AMERICA

Gulf of
Mexico

SOUTH
AMERICA

Key
Katrina's route
wind speed increasing →

tropical   hurricane
storm

• city

**Katrina's diary
(23 – 31 August 2005)**

① Starts on Tuesday 23 August over the Bahamas, as a tropical storm.

② Moves northeast, and grows stronger, over the next 48 hours.

③ At 6.30 pm on Thursday evening, hits the coast of Florida as a category 1 hurricane. Quickly turns south west. Passes over the city of Miami (9 killed), and Everglades National Park.

④ Back over warm water, in the Gulf of Mexico, Katrina gains strength. By 5 am on Saturday it has grown to category 3.

⑤ By 7 am on Sunday, it has reached category 5.

⑥ On Monday 29 August, at 6.10 am, Katrina hits land again, as category 4. It brings death and devastation to Louisana. New Orleans is one of the cities hit.

⑦ Katrina is still heading north – but getting weaker. It is downgraded around here to a tropical storm.

⑧ By late Tuesday, Katrina has weakened to a depression.

⑨ By 11 pm Wednesday 31 August, the last traces of Katrina are dying out, in Canada – but still causing heavy rain and floods!

New Orleans: a city at risk

Look at this map. You can see that New Orleans has a high flood risk!

It is on low land; in fact much of it is below sea level. It is on the edge of a lake, near the coast. There are lakes and swampland all around it. And the Mississippi River runs through it, carrying tonnes of water.

Embankments or **levees** were built to protect New Orleans from floods. But as you'll see next, they could not cope with Katrina.

How Katrina wrecked New Orleans

On Sunday, 28 August, with Katrina on the way, the 3 million residents of New Orleans were told to leave town. 'Anyone who can should go now', said the Mayor. 'There is big trouble ahead. We can't rely on the levees.'

So people went. All day long the airport was packed, and traffic jams blocked the streets, as people left town.

But not all went. Some were too ill, or poor, or frail. Some felt safer at home. Some were afraid to go, in case their homes got robbed. For the people who could not or would not leave, the Louisiana Superdome – a giant sports centre – was turned into a shelter.

Katrina arrives

Early on Monday 29 August, Katrina reached New Orleans. The eye did not pass directly overhead. Even so, the city was battered by raging winds and rain, and a huge storm surge of sea water. Several levees gave way.

There were power cuts all over the city. The roads in and out of it were flooded. So help was very slow to arrive.

Eventually, rescue workers began to search flooded streets and homes for survivors. They took them to the Superdome. But conditions there were horrible by now: over 20 000 people, power cuts, little fresh water, rain leaking in, not enough food, and toilets not working.

By Wednesday August 31, water was still pouring into New Orleans. Over 80% of the city was now flooded. Dead bodies floated in the debris. And armed gangs roamed, looting from shops and homes.

So everyone was ordered out, except repair crews. Buses carried people from the Superdome to shelters in other cities. By Sunday September 4, New Orleans was almost empty. And over 700 people were dead.

Compiled from local news reports.

By 28 August 2006, one year later, much of New Orleans was still in ruins. And half of the city's population had not yet returned.

▲ *September 2: these people are still waiting for buses to get them out of town.*

Your turn

1 Look at the satellite image of Katrina on page 73.
   a About how wide was the storm system?
   b It battered New Orleans, even though the eye did not pass directly over the city. Explain why.

2 Katrina lived for about 200 hours, in different forms.
   a So about what speed did it travel, on average?
   b Suggest a reason why it did not go in a straight line.

3 Look at the photo on page 58. It shows a street in New Orleans, soon after Katrina had passed. You are a reporter. You were at the scene. Write a radio report about what you saw.

4 Now they are rebuilding New Orleans in the same place. Is that a good idea? Write a letter to a newspaper giving your opinion, and reasons.

The big picture

This chapter is about different **climates** around the Earth and the **ecosystems** linked to them. These are the big ideas behind the chapter:

◆ You can divide the Earth into big regions with different climates.

◆ Different climates lead to different ecosystems (plants, animals, and their natural environment).

◆ Ecosystems are fragile. We humans can (and do) harm them.

Your goals for this chapter

By the end of this chapter you should be able to answer these questions:

◆ What do these terms mean?

  climate   *climate region*   *ecosystem*   *biome*   *adapt*

◆ Which factors influence climate? Which is the main one?

◆ What examples can I give, of different climate regions? (At least four.)

◆ Why do different climate regions have different plants and animals?

◆ Which deserts can I name, and where are they? (At least four.)

◆ What is the climate like, in the hot desert ecosystem?

◆ What do these terms mean?

  nocturnal   *nomad*   *pastoralist*   *groundwater*   *oasis*

◆ What examples can I give, of how plants and animals (including humans) have adapted to the climate in the hot desert? (At least six.)

◆ Where will I find tundra, and what kind of climate does it have?

◆ What do these terms mean?

  permafrost   *indigenous*

◆ What examples can I give, of how plants and animals (including humans) have adapted to the climate in the tundra? (At least six.)

◆ How can people harm ecosystems? (At least three ways.)

◆ What is global warming, and why is it the biggest threat to ecosystems?

And then …

When you finish the chapter, come back to this page and see if you have met your goals!

Did you know?

◆ Around 30 of the world's countries are mostly desert.

Did you know?

◆ The driest place on Earth is the Atacama desert in Chile.

Did you know?

◆ Insects in the tundra, (around the North Pole) have anti-freeze in their blood … to stop them freezing.

Did you know?

◆ Snakes are cold-blooded, so they like living in the desert …

◆ … but you won't find any around the North Pole.

Your chapter starter

Look at the photo on page 76.

What's all that stuff on the ground?

What living things can you see in the photo?

There aren't many plants. Can you think why?

That's a city, up ahead. Why do you think it got built there?

Home, camel.

Climate and climate factors

In this unit you will learn what climate is, and why it is so different in different places.

What is climate

Climate is the average weather in a place. It's what the weather is *usually* like there. It can be very different in different places. For example ...

... in London the average maximum temperature for August is 21 °C, and the average rainfall is 59 mm.

But at Giza near Cairo in Egypt, the average maximum temperature for August is 35 °C. And rainfall is zero!

The factors that influence climate

Climate depends on many factors. We'll start with the main one.

1 Latitude – the main factor

The further you go from the equator the cooler it gets. That's because the Earth is curved.

Look at A. These rays from the sun heat the area around the equator. The Earth gets hottest here.

Now look at B. Because the Earth is curved, these rays are spread over a larger area – which means it gets less hot.

C covers an even larger area – so this hardly even gets warm!

So that is why:

◆ the UK is always cooler than Egypt.

◆ Scotland is cooler than the south of England.

◆ it is very cold at the North and South Poles.

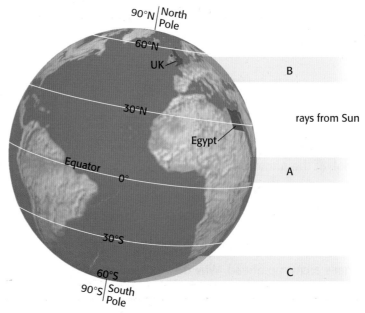

So latitude is the most important factor that influences the climate.
But all these affect it too:

2 Altitude

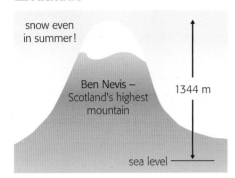

… or height above sea level.
The higher a place is, the cooler it
is. The temperature falls by about
1 °C for every 100 metres you rise.

3 Distance from the sea

The sea is cooler than land in
summer, and warmer in winter. So
a sea breeze keeps the coast cool
in summer – and warm in winter!

4 Prevailing wind direction

For example in the UK the
prevailing wind is from the south
west. It brings water vapour from
the ocean – and that means rain!

5 Ocean currents

For example a warm ocean current
called the **North Atlantic Drift**
warms the west coast of the UK in
winter, by warming the wind.

6 Shelter

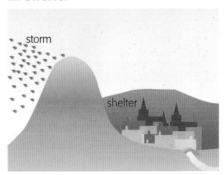

One area may be warm and dry
because it is sheltered by
mountains. Another may be
exposed to the wind and rain.

7 How built up a place is

Concrete stores up heat. Cars and
central heating give out heat. So
a city tends to be warmer than the
countryside around it.

Your turn

1 The *latitude* and *altitude* of a place both influence its
climate. Explain the words in italics. (Glossary?)

2 Draw a spider map to show the factors that influence
climate. You could use a symbol for each factor.

3 Using the map on page 127, give *two* reasons why:
   a Aberdeen is colder than Plymouth, in winter
   b It's colder up Ben Nevis than in Plymouth
   c London is warmer than Belfast, in summer.

4 In the UK, the *prevailing wind* is a south west wind.
   a What does that statement mean? (Glossary?)
   b Explain how this wind affects the climate.

5 Suppose the prevailing wind in the UK was a north
wind. How do you think this would affect the climate?

6 This is about the effect of *distance from the coast*.

In an oven, soil heats up faster than water. When you
take them out of the oven, the soil cools faster too.
Using this idea, and the map on page 129, explain why:
   a Tehran is hotter than Lisbon in summer
   b Lisbon is warmer than Tehran in winter.

7 Now design and draw a diagram to explain why it is
warmer in winter by the coast than it is inland.

8 Here's a challenge! Try to explain why it gets colder
as you go up a mountain.

Climate around the world

Here you will find out how climate varies around the world, and give reasons why.

A world climate map

This map shows the world's **climate regions**.
The key tells you what the climate in each region is like.

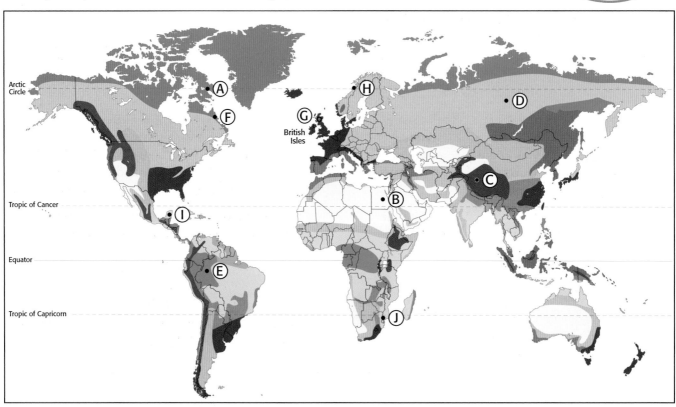

These different climate regions are all the result of the climate factors you met in Unit 6.1.

Look at the dark green region along the equator. The key shows that this region is hot and wet all year.

It is hot because the sun's rays are strongest at the equator. And it is wet because the hot air rises fast, its water vapour condenses to form clouds – and the rain pours down.

Now look at the place marked **A** on the map. What is the climate like here? Can you explain why?

It varies within regions

The map shows that Scotland is in a region of warm summers, mild winters, and rain all year.

But this does not mean that all of Scotland has the same climate. For example, high places like the Cairngorms have cool summers and very cold winters, often with lots of snow. But *overall*, Scotland has quite a mild climate.

In the same way, the climate within other regions varies too.

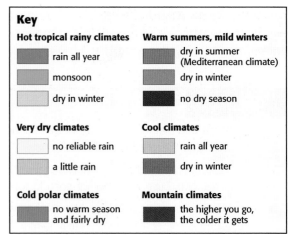

Key

Hot tropical rainy climates
- rain all year
- monsoon
- dry in winter

Very dry climates
- no reliable rain
- a little rain

Cold polar climates
- no warm season and fairly dry

Warm summers, mild winters
- dry in summer (Mediterranean climate)
- dry in winter
- no dry season

Cool climates
- rain all year
- dry in winter

Mountain climates
- the higher you go, the colder it gets

Your turn

1 See if you can explain the difference between *weather* and *climate*. (Glossary?)

2 Look at the map on page 80.
What is the climate like at the place marked:
a **B**?   b **D**?   c **E**?

3 Look again at the map on page 80. It is a lot cooler at **D** than at **B**. Suggest a reason.

4 Now look at the map below. It shows the world's main mountain ranges, and *some* winds and ocean currents.
a What are *ocean currents*? (Glossary?)
b There is a warm current to the west of the UK. It is called …? (Unit 6.1.)
c i Using the map on page 128 to help you, name a country that may be affected by a cold current.
   ii In what way might that country be affected?
d Now name a country where the prevailing wind is:
   i from the south east   ii from the north west

5 Below are some facts about places marked on the map on page 80. See if you can explain them, by comparing that map with the map below.
a It is cold all year round at **C**.
b **G** is at the same latitude as **F**, but is warmer.
c **A** is at the same latitude as **H**, but is colder.
d It is cooler and wetter at **I** than at **B**.
e It is drier at **B** than at **H**.

6 Now look at this graph. It is a **climate graph** for a place called Frobisher Bay. The blue numbers and bars show rainfall. The red numbers and red line show temperature.

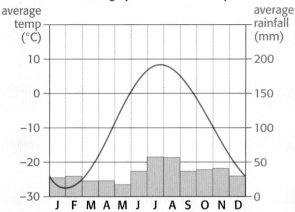

Climate graph for Frobisher Bay

Try these questions about the climate in Frobisher Bay.
a Which two months are usually the wettest?
b Which month is driest?
c What is the average rainfall in August?
d Which month is warmest?
e For how many months of the year is it freezing?

7 Frobisher Bay is shown by a letter on the map on page 80. Which letter is it: **A**, **B**, **G** or **J**?

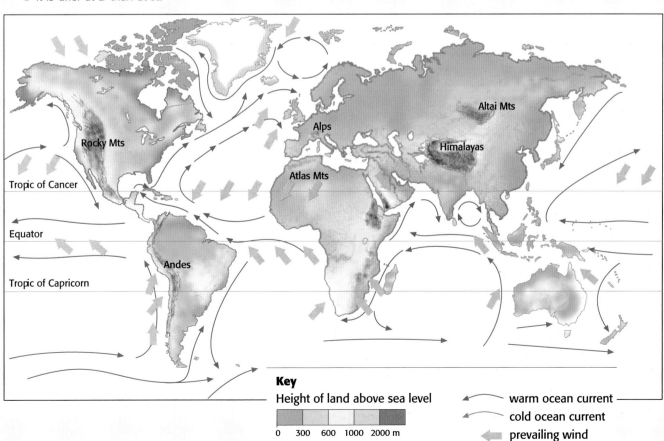

Key

Height of land above sea level

0   300   600   1000   2000 m

⟵ warm ocean current
⟵ cold ocean current
⟸ prevailing wind

Rocky Mts
Tropic of Cancer
Equator
Andes
Tropic of Capricorn
Alps
Atlas Mts
Himalayas
Altai Mts

Climate and ecosystems

In this unit you will learn what ecosystems are, and how they relate to climate.

Scenes from different climate regions

Look at these photos. They are from four different climate regions.
Look how different the places are.

This is a **hot desert**, in the hot dry climate region. What do you notice about the vegetation (plants) in this place? What animal can you see?

Hot desert

Looks familiar? It is **deciduous forest**, found in the climate region with warm summers, mild winters, and rain all year. It's the one the UK belongs to.

Deciduous forest

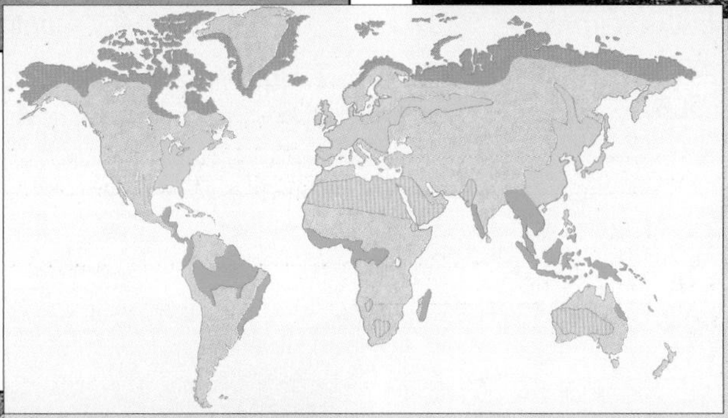

Key
- hot desert
- Arctic tundra
- tropical rainforest
- deciduous forest

Tropical rainforest

Tundra

Tropical rainforests are found in the hot wet climate region, where it is hot and wet all year. You'll see animals such as monkeys and parrots.

This shows **tundra**, in the cold dry polar climate region. The soil below the surface is permanently frozen.

They are all ecosystems

Those four photos on page 82 show different **ecosystems**.
An ecosystem is made up of:

◆ living things (plant, animals) and
◆ the surroundings or **environment** they live in – the air, water, soil, and the climate (how warm or wet it is).

A garden pond is a small ecosystem. A rainforest is a large one.
All the Earth's rainforests together make up a very large ecosystem.
All the hot deserts make up another.
These very large ecosytems are often called **biomes**.

Did you know?
◆ Humans adapt quickly to different climates ...
◆ ... with the help of things like heaters, thick coats, shorts, sunglasses ...

Why are they so different?

The ecosystems in the photos are very different – and it's all because of the climate.

Look at this diagram:

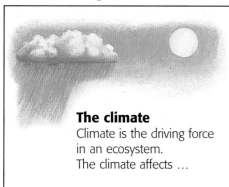

The climate
Climate is the driving force in an ecosystem.
The climate affects ...

Later you will see how plants and animals (including humans) have adapted to the climate in two ecosystems that are very dry – but very different: hot deserts and tundra.

1 the soil
How thick and rich the soil is depends partly on the climate. Rock breaks down fast into soil in a hot damp climate.

which affects ...

2 the vegetation (plants and trees)
It **adapts** to suit the climate and soil. Vegetation grow fastest and thickest in a hot damp sunny climate.

which affects ...

3 the animals
They **adapt** to cope with the climate, and to feed on the plants or each other.

---

1 Explain what this term means. (Check the glossary?)
  a ecosystem   b biome   c adapts
2 Do you think a school playing field counts as an ecosystem? What plants and animals would you find there? (Insects are animals!)
3 Now choose one photo from page 82. Describe the scene fully, for someone who can't see the photo.
4 Look again at the photos. Of the four places:
  a which one would you most like to be in? Why?
  b which one would you least like to be in? Why?
5 Look at these climate graphs. They match two of the ecosystems on page 82.
  a One is for the deciduous forest ecosystem. Which one?
  b Which ecosystem does the other graph match?

Climate graph A

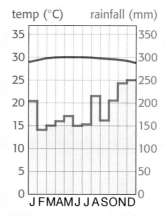

Climate graph B

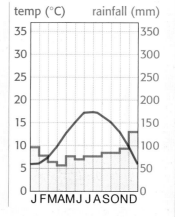

Here you will find out what deserts are, and where they are.

What is a desert?

A **desert** is a region that gets less than 25 cm of rain a year.
Some deserts are hot. Some are cool. Some are very cold. But all are dry!

This map shows the world's deserts. Notice where the hot deserts are.

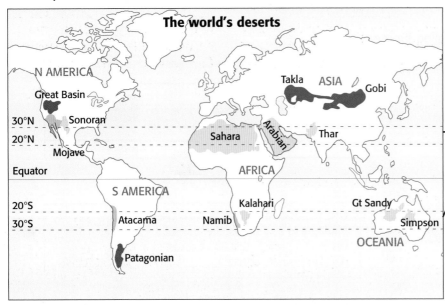

The hot deserts lie in bands on each side of the equator, roughly between 20° and 30°.

Key
☐ hot desert
▨ cool coastal desert
▨ cold desert

Why are they so dry?

Scotland gets quite a lot of rain. Tropical rainforests get buckets of rain. Why do the deserts get so little? The answer is different for different deserts. So let's start with the hot ones.

Why the hot deserts are dry

Look at this diagram:

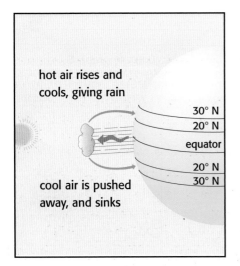

hot air rises and cools, giving rain

30° N
20° N
equator
20° N
30° N

cool air is pushed away, and sinks

1 The sun is strongest at the equator. So the warm damp air at the equator rises fast. It cools, clouds form – and the rain pours down around the equator.

2 High up, the cooled air gets pushed away as more air rises. It sinks to Earth in the area between 20° and 30°. It has little moisture left – and warms as it sinks. So no clouds form, and no rain. The result: desert!

3 No clouds means the sky is clear in this area. So it gets very hot in the day, when the sun shines. And very cold at night. (Clouds keep heat in).

So the hot deserts are dry – but not *always* hot! Thanks to clear cloudless skies, temperatures can reach over 50 °C in the day – and plunge to below freezing at night.

Why the other deserts are dry

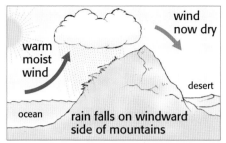 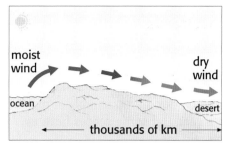 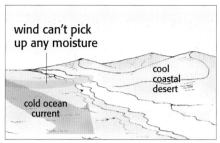

Some deserts are dry because they are sheltered from the rain by large mountain ranges, like this one.

Some are very far from the sea. By the time it reaches them, the wind has already lost all its water vapour.

And some are dry because cold ocean currents prevent the wind from picking up any moisture.

The sky over these deserts will also be clear and cloudless – so the temperature will plunge at night.

And are they all just sand?

No. Deserts have some sand – but they have more rock and stones than sand. This shows where the sand comes from:

 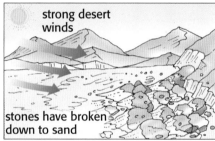 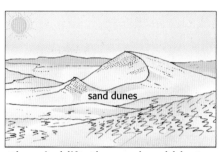

Rock cools and contracts at night, as the desert cools. It expands again in the day. Over time, this breaks it into stones.

Stones cool down and heat up too, and break into smaller pieces. The wind knocks them against the rock, and each other, giving sand.

The wind lifts the sand and blasts everything with it. It also carries sand away, and deposits it in more sheltered places, as sand dunes.

But you will not see much soil in the desert – because soil needs rain! (Soil forms when air and rain react with the minerals in rock and stones, and break them down.)

Your turn

1 Look at the map of the deserts, on page 84.
  a Which is the world's largest desert?
  b Name four of the countries that share it. (Page 129?)
  c Name: i a cold desert ii three deserts with coasts

2 With help from the map on pages 128–129, name:
  a a desert in China   b a desert in southern Africa
  c a desert in Pakistan   d a desert in South America

3 The Gobi desert is colder than the Thar. Why?

4 Using the information above, and the map on page 81, see if you can explain why these get so little rain:
  a the Atacama desert   b the Gobi desert

5 Below is some climate data for a place in the Sahara.
  a In which month is that place: i hottest? ii driest?
  b Sometimes the road into it gets flooded! In which month is this most likely to happen?

6 a Now draw a climate graph for that place. (Page 81.)
  b The people in that place divide the year into summer and winter. Which do you think are the summer months? Use your graph to help you decide.

Month	J	F	M	A	M	J	J	A	S	O	N	D
Average temp (°C)	13	15	20	23	26	27	28	27	25	21	16	13
Average rainfall (mm)	3	3	5	9	15	18	42	70	48	21	0	2

The hot desert ecosystem

Here you will find out how plants and animals have adapted to the climate in the hot deserts.

Life in a harsh climate

As you saw in the last unit, the hot deserts have a very harsh climate. Temperatures can reach up to 50 °C in the day, and drop sharply at night. The rainfall is always less than 250 mm a year. But some places have as little as 15 mm – and some have had no rain for years.

All plants and animals need water. And if they get too hot, they die. Even so, the hot desert is home to *hundreds* of species of plants and animals. Amazing!

So how do they survive? They have all adapted in different ways to cope with the hot dry climate. Let's look at some examples.

How have plants adapted?

Some plants are **succulents**, which means they can store water inside themselves when it rains. This one, the **euphorbia**, stores water in its leaves. (It is like a cactus.)

Large areas of desert have **groundwater** in rock below the surface. Some plants, like this one, have very long roots, 8 or 9 metres long, that grow down to find it.

Some plants sprout and live for just a short time, after rain. They produce seeds with a waterproof coat, that can survive, without drying out, until the next rain.

▶ Hardy grass also grows in the desert. The thin leaves reduce water loss. But in the driest parts of the desert you can go for miles without seeing any plants.

How have animals adapted?

Like plants, animals have adapted in different ways:

◆ behaviour. Some hide away in the hot day, and come out at night when it's cooler. Animals that do this are called **nocturnal**.

◆ body shape. Small bodies can stay cooler. So most desert animals are small. But long tails, legs and ears help to lose body heat.

◆ use of water. Some animals don't need much water. Some can store it up. Some lose very little in urine or sweat.

Look at these examples:

The **camel** stores water in its blood. It stores fat in its hump, for energy. It can go for up to two weeks without a drink, and even longer without food. (It will eat cactus, grass, seeds, tents …)

The **jerboa** lives in a burrow, and is nocturnal. It gets enough water from its food (seeds, plants, insects). Long strong back legs help it hop a long way for food (and to escape).

The **fennec fox** is also nocturnal. It can go for a long time without water. It will eat anything (jerboa, plants, seeds, lizards, insects, birds). Those big ears keep it cool – and help it hear food, and enemies!

Lizards and **snakes** are cold-blooded, so come out in the sun to get warm. Their thick skins help to cut down water loss. They eat small animals, and each other!

The **scorpion** has a hard shell that cuts down water loss. It lives in burrows or under rocks in the day, and hunts at night. It gets water from its food (insects and spiders).

The **houbara bustard** can fly, but usually walks. It can stick out its feathers to cool down. It gets water from its food (jerboa and other rodents, and lizards).

Your turn

1 Some desert plants are *succulents*. Explain that term.

2 Look at the climate table at the bottom of page 85.
 a In which month are plants likely to grow best? Why?
 b In which month are fennec foxes least likely to come out during the day? Why?

3 Some desert plants have shallow roots that spread widely. See if you can think of a reason.

4 The wild animals you find in the hot desert are very different from those in the UK. Why is this?

5 Smaller animals can stay cooler. Try to explain why!

Humans in the hot deserts

Here you will learn how humans have adapted to living in the hot deserts.

Coping with the hot deserts

People have been living in the hot deserts for thousands of years. (But the deserts are still quite empty compared to most places.)

We can adapt to hot climates by wearing cool clothes, and living in cool dwellings. But we still need food and water. So how do desert people cope? Finding water is the key.

Finding water in the hot desert

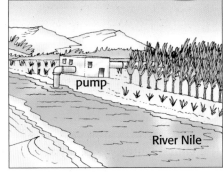

There is **groundwater** below much of the desert – from the time it was green, rainy and fertile, long ago. In some places, you can reach the water by digging a well.	In some places the groundwater is very close to the surface. These places are called **oases**. Vegetation grows easily here. Wells are easy to dig – or there may be a spring.	Some deserts even have rivers through them. In Egypt, the River Nile runs through the Sahara. You can pipe water from the river to the land on each side.

Some desert dwellers are **nomads**, always moving from place to place. But they never get *too* far from a well or oasis. Others settle down near water.

On the move: the nomads

Merchants

Some nomads are **merchants**. They cross the desert from place to place, carrying goods to trade. In the past, they used camel trains, and carried salt, gold, ivory, spices, and even slaves. Some still use camels but many have switched to trucks. They may carry household goods, cloth, dates, tinned foods, and even tourists!

Pastoralists

Other nomads are **pastoralists**. They rear camels, goats, sheep and cattle, and sell them at markets. They live on their milk and meat. (They don't eat much camel meat, since camels are used for transport.)

The pastoralists move around with their animals, to find grass. They live in goatskin tents, which they just roll up and take with them. A family can pack all it owns onto a couple of camels.

Pastoralists travel in small groups, and set up camp together in new places. But if there is not much grass, they soon move on. They store water in goatskins, and fill them up when they reach a well. They use camel dung as a fuel for cooking.

▲ *A nomad camp in the Sahara. These people belong to the Tuareg tribe.*

Settling down: life in an oasis

Most desert dwellers live in oases. Some oases are just tiny villages, but others have towns, and even cities.

Because of the water, oasis dwellers can grow a good variety of crops – oranges, peaches, dates, figs, wheat, barley…

Life in an oasis is easier than life on the move, especially if the rains fail and there is no grass for your animals to eat. That's why many desert pastoralists are now starting to settle down in oases.

Other desert dwellers

Many deserts are rich in natural resources. For example the deserts of the Arabian peninsula (where Saudi Arabia is – see page 129) hold over half the world's oil. Settlements are built around the oil fields, and workers are brought in. Water supplies are laid on for them.

Bringing water to the desert

Now people are moving more and more water around, to help them cope in the hot deserts.

From rivers
In some places, people pipe water into the desert, to grow crops. For example, Egypt has turned over 7000 sq km of the Sahara into farmland, by **irrigating** it with Nile water.

From under the ground
Most of Libya is in the Sahara. (Look for it on the map on page 129.) Some parts of Libya *never* get rain. But today, Libyans enjoy pure clear water, pumped up from giant **aquifers** of groundwater under the desert. Some is piped to the cities for drinking, and some is used for crops.

From the sea
The countries in the Arabian peninsula are mostly desert. Most are wealthy because of oil, and most have a coastline. So they turn sea water into fresh water by removing the salt from it (**desalination**). They pump the fresh water into the desert for growing crops, and other projects.

▲ *A Tuareg farmer at work in an oasis in the Sahara in Algeria.*

Your turn

1 Not many people live in the hot deserts. Why not?

2 In the Sahara, the population density is 2 people per square kilometre.
  a What does *population density* mean? (Glossary?)
  b So does that mean you will find two people living in each square kilometre of the desert? Explain.

3 In many places, the desert has groundwater below it.
  a What is *groundwater*?
  b How did it get there? (There is a clue on page 86.)
  c It is very important, for the desert dwellers. Why?
  d Some of it is in huge *aquifers*. What are these? (Look in the glossary.)

4 Explain these terms:
  a nomad   b pastoralist   c oasis

5 Look at the climate table at the bottom of page 85.
  a Which month do you think the pastoralists like best?
  b Which may be the most difficult months for them?

6 a Most places in the hot desert have little or no soil. Why is this? (Page 85?)
  b But there *is* some farming in the desert. Explain.

7 Now look back at the photo on page 76. You are one of the people in the lower left, heading for the city. (It is Aswan, in the Sahara in Egypt.) Describe what you see around you, and how you are feeling.

The Arctic tundra

Here you will find out what, and where, the Arctic tundra ecosystem is – and how living things have adapted to the harsh conditions there.

What is the Arctic tundra?

The Arctic tundra is the ecosystem that lies up around the north pole:

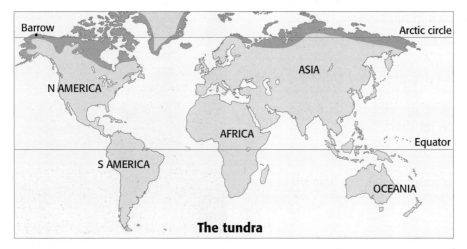

The tundra

▲ *A polar bear on the frozen tundra.*

What is it like there?

◆ Winters are long, cold and dark. The average temperature is around – 30 °C. By mid-December it is dark all day.

◆ Summers are very cool (3 ° to 12 °C) and short, but with long hours of daylight. By mid-July it is light for 24 hours a day.

◆ It is dry. There is less than 25 cm a year of rain or snow.

◆ There are harsh, biting winds.

◆ It is so cold that most of the soil is frozen solid all year round. It is called **permafrost**. But the top layer of soil thaws for 2 or 3 months every summer. Then plants grow quickly, covering it in a green carpet.

◆ There are no trees, because they can't grow roots into the permafrost.

◆ When it does rain, or the top layer of soil thaws, the water can't soak away through the permafrost. So bogs, streams and ponds appear in summer, giving plenty of water for the plants and animals.

Plants of the tundra

The tundra is a harsh place. Even so, it is is home to many species of plants and animals. (But not as many as in the hot desert.)

Plants need warmth, and sunlight for **photosynthesis**. So how have they adapted to the cold, and the long spells of low light? Like this:

◆ They can carry out photosynthesis at low temperatures, in low light – even when covered with snow!

◆ They grow low to the ground, and close together, for protection against the cold and wind.

◆ The growing season is short, so they grow fast. Some send out underground stems or **runners** that sprout new plants, instead of forming flowers and seeds.

▲ *The tundra in summer. Look at the ponds. These animals are reindeer (also called caribou).*

▲ *Some tundra flowers.*

Animals

The animals of the tundra include:

◆ **carnivores** or meat-eating animals such as brown bears and Arctic foxes
◆ **herbivores** such as musk ox and reindeer (caribou), that feed on plants
◆ birds and insects.

Here are some of the ways animals have adapted to the harsh climate:

◆ Many have a thick outer coat of coarse waterproof fur to keep them dry, plus an inner coat of fluffy hair to trap heat.
◆ Many build up a thick layer of fat, ready for winter.
◆ Short legs, tails and snouts help to cut down heat loss.
◆ Some move in the winter. The birds fly south to warmer climates. Reindeer move to where they can find lichen, their winter food.

Look at these examples:

Tundra swans escape from the winter cold. Every year they fly up to 6000 km south, to warmer coastal areas in the USA.

The brown bear has a thick coat. It grows a thick layer of fat for winter. It digs a den and stays inside for the coldest months.

Musk oxen have thick shaggy coats, with fluffy hair underneath. Short legs help to reduce heat loss. They huddle for warmth and safety.

The Arctic fox has shorter legs, tail, ears and snout than British foxes, to reduce heat loss. Its thick coat goes white in winter to help it hide.

Your turn

1 a Name five countries with tundra. (Pages 128 –129?)
  b Which country has the world's largest area of tundra?

2 This climate graph is for the town of Barrow, in the tundra in Alaska. (It is marked on the map on page 90.)
  a In which month does the top layer of soil start thawing?
  b Which months are the growing season for plants?
  c In which month are you likely to find most water in ponds and bogs? Explain.
  d In which months does the permafrost thaw out?
  e In which months does *snow* fall?
  f Musk oxen dig under ice and snow for food, with their hooves. In which months do they need to do that?
  g Tundra swans leave the tundra in early October, flying south. They are back again by mid-May. So what sort of temperatures are *too low* for the tundra swans?

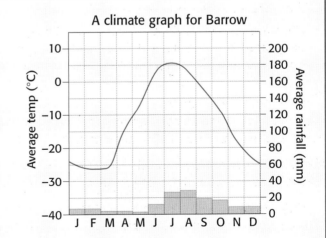

A climate graph for Barrow

3 a Now draw up a table to help you compare the climates in the hot deserts and tundra – and fill it in!
  b In which way are those two ecosystems alike?
  c What is the *really big* difference between them?

Humans in the Arctic tundra

Here you'll learn about the people who live in the Arctic tundra, and what they do there.

Who lives there?

Bitter cold, biting winds, frozen ground, months of darkness. How could anyone survive in the Arctic tundra? About 4 million people do!

Two main groups of people live there:

◆ the **indigenous** people, whose ancestors have been there for thousands of years.

◆ descendants of people who arrived within the last 400 years or so. (Lots of new people have arrived in the last 30 or 40 years.)

The second group outnumber the indigenous people, by about 9 to 1.

The indigenous people of the tundra

The first arrivals

The first people arrived in the tundra about 10 000 years ago. They were hunters and gatherers, and found plenty to hunt there. Reindeer, musk ox, woolly mammoth. Seal and walrus at the coast. Fish in the icy rivers. And in the short summers, they could gather berries and seeds.

They lived a **nomadic** life, following the wild animals. They lived in rough shelters. They dried the meat and fish they caught, and stored it for the dark winter months. They wore the animal skins and furs to keep warm.

Then, perhaps around 7000 years ago, they began to herd reindeer for meat and milk. They moved around with them looking for pasture.

The indigenous people today

The descendants of those early settlers still live in the tundra. There are many different groups. (The list on the right shows just some of them.) They speak different languages. But they all share a tradition of hunting, fishing, and herding reindeer.

▲ *A little Nenets girl with her two puppies, outside her tent home in the tundra in Siberia, northern Russia.*

Some indigenous people of the tundra

◆ In Canada and the USA:
  Inuit
  Inuvialuit
◆ In Greenland:
  Inuit
◆ In Scandinavia:
  Sami
◆ In Russia:
  Nenets
  Enets
  Sami
  Selkups

Did you know?
◆ *The indigenous people of the Arctic tundra used to be called Eskimos.*
◆ *Many now find this name insulting.*

▶ *A reindeer herder in the tundra in Siberia, northern Russia. Herders can look after thousands of reindeer.*

How their lives are changing

Life is changing for the indigenous people.

◆ Many still live by hunting and fishing. But instead of sleds and spears they now go by snowmobile, use guns and fishing rods – and live in houses.

◆ Some are still nomads, living in tents and herding reindeer.

◆ But some live in towns and cities in the tundra. They may find work in factories, or on oil fields, or on fishing boats. (Many find it hard to get other work, because they did not spend much time at school.)

The later arrivals

Here are some of the later arrivals:

◆ In the 17th and 18th century, fur traders and trappers arrived, and missionaries, and whalers, and people hoping to find gold.

◆ People moved in to 'run' the tundra areas for their governments.

◆ In the last 40 years or so, oil and mining companies have arrived, looking for oil, gas, and metal ores.

Conflicts in the tundra

The Russian tundra is especially rich in minerals. Large areas of reindeer pastures have been taken over for mining, and oil and gas production, and new towns to support these.

The air, land and rivers are being polluted by waste from mining. The new roads and railways scare animals away, and upset their migration patterns. This is causing conflict with the indigenous people.

Oil is also big business in the tundra in Alaska, USA. The oil is moved from the oil fields in the **Trans-Alaska pipeline**, 1300 km long, which runs across the tundra to a port.

Oil has leaked from this pipe from time to time. People worry about the pollution – and they also fear that oil production may start in other parts of the Alaskan tundra, that are protected at the moment.

But as you will see next, these are not the biggest threats the tundra faces.

▲ *Inuit children being collected from school by snowmobile, in the tundra in Canada.*

▲ *Fumes from metal smelting in Norilsk, a mining city in the Russian tundra. It's inside the Arctic circle.*

Your turn

1 The Arctic tundra covers an area of about 12 million square kilometres. About 4 million people live in it.
  a Work out the population density there. (Glossary?)
  b How does this compare with the population density
    i in the Sahara desert? ii in the UK? (Page 88.)
  c The deserts and tundra are often called 'empty lands'. Do you agree with that description?

2 a What does the term *indigenous people* mean?
  b Name one tribe of indigenous people of the tundra.
  c The indigenous people did not grow crops. Why not?

3 Look at the first photo on page 92. What do you think the family does for water, and heating?

4 Many reindeer herders live in tents like the one at the top of page 92. They travel with their reindeer between summer and winter grazing areas. Do you think this is an easy way of life? What difficulties might there be? (Is darkness one of them?)

5 Compare the reindeer herders with the herders of camels and goats in the desert.
  a What do they have in common?
  b What would you say is the biggest difference in their way of life?

6 Many new arrivals to the tundra are miners. What special dfficulties might miners face?

Ecosystems under threat

In this unit you will learn about ways in which our activities threaten ecosystems – with hot deserts and the Arctic tundra as examples.

Clever us!

We humans are very clever. We have spread all over the Earth. We have invaded nearly every ecosystem. We have adapted to them through our clothing, and shelters, and what we eat.

And everywhere we go, we have managed to exploit plants, and other animals, and water, rocks and minerals, for our benefit.

But the trouble is ...

The trouble is, we have often harmed the places we invaded. We have destroyed many other species. By the time we notice, it is often too late to repair the damage. So perhaps we are not so clever after all.

Remember, an ecosystem is the living things *and* their non-living environment: water, air, soil, climate. We can harm all of those. Let's see some examples.

Threats to the hot desert ecosystem

These are some of the threats to the hot desert ecosystem:

◆ **Extraction of oil and gas, and other minerals**. We need these. But animals are driven out when the ground gets dug up, and roads are built, and traffic begins. And often the place gets polluted with leaks from pipes, and poisonous waste.

◆ **Using up the groundwater**. The groundwater below the desert is often called **fossil water** because it has been there for thousands of years. As the population of oases grows, the fossil water gets used up faster. It can't be replaced. One day, this could mean the end of some oases.

◆ **Hunting.** The numbers of many desert animals have fallen fast, thanks to hunting. In the Sahara, these include the houbara bustard. Sometimes the hunters are wealthy tourists!

▲ Oil production in the remote desert in Saudi Arabia. The oil is carried away by pipeline.

▲ Exposed permafrost in the tundra. (It's the pale grey strip.) It starts to thaw once it is exposed.

▶ Hunters in the tundra.

Threats to the Arctic tundra ecosystem

◆ **Extraction of oil, and gas and other minerals**. As in the hot deserts, animals and people are driven off the land when mines, oil fields, and gas fields are developed, and new towns built.

◆ **Disturbance of the permafrost.** The low plants that cover the ground in the tundra help to protect the permafrost. If the vegetation is cleared away, the permafrost starts to thaw. And then the ground collapses.

Once permafrost thaws, plants will grow well – for a time. But now when it rains, the rain soaks away through the soil. Soon no plants grow well, even in summer, because there is not enough water.

This is a big problem, since any development (new towns, roads, mines, oilfields) means that vegetation gets cleared away.

◆ **Hunting**. This has lead to a big fall in the numbers of many animals of the tundra, including the brown bear, Arctic fox and musk ox.

▲ *Built on top of the permafrost – and now the permafrost is thawing, thanks to global warming.*

The biggest threat of all: global warming

The Earth is getting warmer. Most experts agree that we are causing this (or at the very least speeding it up). Here is how:

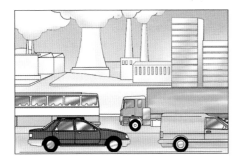

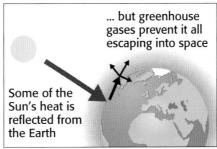

... but greenhouse gases prevent it all escaping into space

Some of the Sun's heat is reflected from the Earth

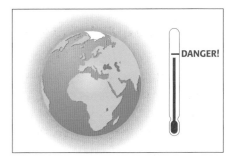

DANGER!

We are burning up more and more fossil fuel – coal, oil and natural gas – around the world. This produces carbon dioxide ...

... which is a **greenhouse gas**. That means it helps to trap heat around the Earth, and stop it escaping into space.

The more carbon dioxide in the air, the warmer the Earth becomes. The result is that climates all over the world are changing.

Plants and animals adapt to the climate. But if they can't adapt quickly enough when it changes, they will die out. We can't tell how the plants and animals of the desert and tundra will respond – but it will be the end for some.

The news gets worse. As the tundra warms up, the permafrost will melt. And release massive amounts of carbon dioxide and methane gases (from rotting vegetation) that have been locked up in it for thousands of years. Methane is an even more powerful greenhouse gas than carbon dioxide. So global warming will get faster.

Your turn

1 a Three of the threats given in this unit affect both the tundra *and* hot deserts. Which three?
b Do you think these are threats in all ecosystems? If yes, see if you can give some examples.

2 When permafrost melts:
a some results are *local*. Try to give two examples.
b some results are *global*. Explain.

3 Why is global warming the biggest threat of all?

▲ Stoer, Scotland.

▲ Morston Marshes, Norfolk.

SCOTLAND

NORTHERN IRELAND

REPUBLIC OF IRELAND

WALES ENGLAND

▲ Sennen Beach, Cornwall.

▲ The Seven Sisters, Sussex.

The big picture

This chapter is all about the **coast**, where the land meets the sea.
These are the big ideas behind the chapter:

◆ The coast is shaped and changed by the waves – and by humans!

◆ The waves shape it by eroding, transporting and depositing material.
The result is special landforms.

◆ We humans also change it, through the way we use the land.

◆ There is a limited amount of coast, and many conflicting demands on
it. So we need to manage and use it in a sustainable way.

◆ In some places around the coast, people's homes and land are
threatened by erosion. We need to respond in a sustainable way.

Did you know?
◆ Part of Britain's south coast is called the Jurassic coast ...
◆ ... because lots of dinosaur remains are found there.

Your goals for this chapter

By the end of this chapter you should be able to answer these questions:

◆ What causes waves?

◆ How do waves shape the coast?

◆ What do these terms mean?
erode   transport   deposit   longshore drift

◆ What are these, and how were they formed?
*beach   bay   headland   cave   arch   stack   stump
wavecut platform   spit   salt marsh*

◆ How do we use the land along the coast, and what kinds of
conflict arise?

◆ What causes cliffs to collapse?

◆ What kinds of things can we do, to protect people's lands and homes
from erosion by the waves?

◆ Why can't we protect all the places that are at risk from erosion?

◆ How can we fight erosion in a sustainable way?

Did you know?
◆ The UK has 12 430 km of coast.
◆ 9911 km of it is in Scotland!
◆ The distance from London to New York: 5530 km!

And then ...

When you finish the chapter, come back to this page and see if you have
met your goals!

Did you know?
◆ 8 of the world's 10 largest cities are on a coast.
◆ Over half the people in the world live within 200 km of a coast.

Your chapter starter

Page 96 shows places on the UK's coast.

What's the coast?

What can you do there?

How far do *you* live from the coast?

Why does it look so different in different places?

Waves and tides

In this unit you'll learn what causes waves and tides, and begin to find out how waves affect the coast.

What causes waves?

Waves are caused by the **wind** dragging on the surface of the water. The length of water the wind blows over is called its **fetch**.

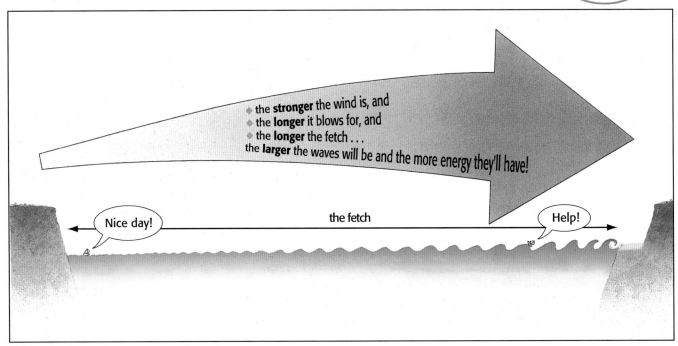

- the **stronger** the wind is, and
- the **longer** it blows for, and
- the **longer** the fetch . . .
the **larger** the waves will be and the more energy they'll have!

Nice day!

the fetch

Help!

When waves reach the coast

Out at sea, the waves roll like this. In a gale they can be over 30 metres high!

Swash this then?

They break in shallow water, like this. The water that rushes up the sand is called the **swash**.

Backwash!

The water rolling back into the sea, like this, is called the **backwash**.

If the backwash has more energy than the swash the waves eat at the land, dragging pebbles and sand away. (This happens with high steep waves.) But if the swash has more energy than the backwash, material is carried on to the land and left there. (This happens with low flat waves.)

Tides

Even when the sea is calm and flat, the water level is always changing. That's mainly because of the moon. As the moon travels around the Earth it attracts the sea and pulls it upwards. (The sun helps too, but it is much further away so its pull is not so strong.)

The rise and fall of the sea gives us the **tides**. Look at these photos:

Tuesday 9.00 am. The tide is **in** at this coastal town. In fact the sea has reached its highest level for today. This is called **high tide**.

Same day, 3.20 pm. Now the tide is **out**, leaving the boats resting on the mud. The sea has fallen to its lowest level for the day. This is called **low tide**.

High tides occur about every twelve and a half hours, with low tides in between. The drop in sea level from high to low tide is called the **tidal range**. It keeps changing, because the pull of the moon and sun changes as the moon moves around the Earth, and the Earth moves around the sun.

Your turn

1 Which three factors determine how high the waves in a place will be?

2 The arrows are winds blowing onto island **X**.

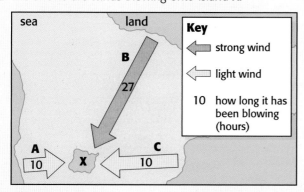

Which wind will produce:
a the largest waves   b the smallest waves
at the coast of **X**? Explain your answers.

3 Now think about the waves around your own island.
   a The *prevailing wind* in the UK is a *south west wind*. What do the terms in italics mean? (Glossary?)
   b Explain why the south west tip of England gets some really high waves. (Check pages 128–129.)

c Most of the UK's surfing schools are in south west England, and Wales. Suggest a reason.

4 Using a full sentence, explain what these terms mean:
   a swash
   b backwash

5 Look at the photos on page 96.
   a Which beach do you think has stronger backwash, **C** or **D**? What is your evidence?
   b Which of the four places probably gets hardly any waves? Explain how you decided.

6 a What are *tides*, and why do they occur?
   b Photo **B** on page 96 was taken at low tide. How would the scene look different, at high tide?
   c Now repeat **b** for photo **C**.
   d Look at photo **D**. Was this taken at high tide? How can you tell?

7 Now look at photo **A** on page 96. You are on holiday near there. Two days ago you were scrambling around on the rocks – and got trapped at **X** by high tide! Write a really exciting entry for your diary saying how you felt, and how you were saved.

The waves at work

In this unit you'll learn how waves shape the coastline.

What do the waves do?

Waves work non-stop, night and day, year after year, shaping the coastline. This shows what they do.

3 They drop or **deposit** it in sheltered areas where they lose energy.

1 They wear away or **erode** the coast. These cliffs are being eroded. (Some of the rock has already been **weathered** – broken down by weather and plants.)

2 They carry away or **transport** the eroded material.

Now we will look at each of these in more detail.

Erosion

This is how waves wear away the coast:

They pound at the rock like a hammer. Over time, this breaks the rock up.

Chunks of rock get knocked together and worn into smaller and smaller bits. This is called **attrition**. They end up as **shingle** (pebbles) and **sand**.

They force water into cracks in the rock. That helps to break it up. It's called **hydraulic action**.

They dissolve soluble material from the rock. This is called **solution**.

They fling sand and pebbles against the rock. These wear it away like sandpaper. This is called **abrasion**.

The more energy the waves have, and the softer the rock, the faster erosion will be.

Transport

The waves carry the eroded material away. Some is carried right out to sea. But a lot is carried *along* the coastline. Like this …

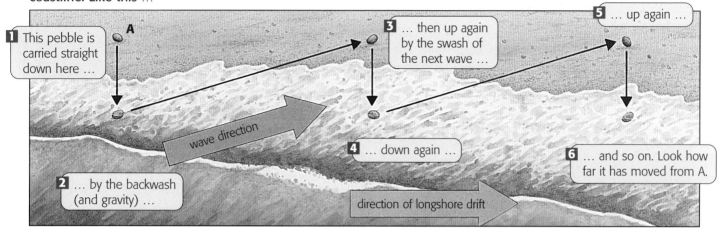

1 This pebble is carried straight down here …

A

2 … by the backwash (and gravity) …

wave direction

3 … then up again by the swash of the next wave …

4 … down again …

direction of longshore drift

5 … up again …

6 … and so on. Look how far it has moved from A.

In this way, hundreds of thousands of tonnes of pebbles and sand get moved along our coastline every year. This movement is called **longshore drift**.

Many seaside towns build **groynes** to stop their beaches being carried away by longshore drift. Look at this photo.

Deposition

Waves continually carry material on and off the land. If they carry more *on* than *off* – a beach forms!

Beaches form in sheltered areas. Low flat waves carry material up the beach and leave it there. Some beaches are made of sand, and some are **shingle** (small pebbles).

a groyne

N

▲ *The groynes stop the beach being carried away.*

Your turn

1 Waves do three jobs that shape the coastline. Name them.

2 Describe three ways in which waves erode rock.

3 These two pebbles are made of the same rock.
   a Which one has been in the water for longer? Explain.
   b Name the process that made Y so smooth.

X   Y

4 Look at the groynes in the photo above.
   a Why were they built?
   b Are they working? How can you tell?
   c From which direction do the waves usually arrive at this beach?
      i from the south west
      ii from the south east
   Give a reason for your choice.

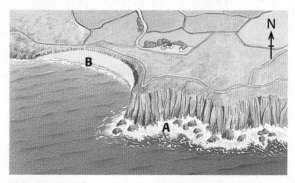

N

B

A

5 This drawing shows part of an island (not Britain).
   a The *prevailing wind* for the island is blowing. From where does it blow? (Look at the waves!)
   b There is no beach at **A**. Suggest a reason.
   c There is a good beach at **B**. Give a reason.
   d Where might the sand at **B** have come from?

6 Do you think the rock around our coast all erodes at the same rate? Explain your answer.

Landforms created by the waves

In this unit you will learn about the landforms that the waves create along the coast, by eroding and depositing material.

Sculptor at work!

This coast is made of different rocks, some hard, some soft. Once upon a time it was straight. Just look at it now!

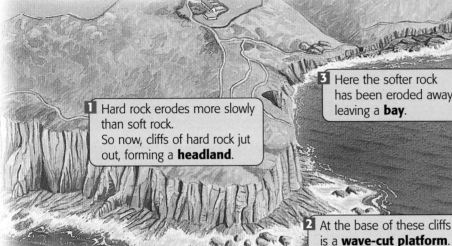

1 Hard rock erodes more slowly than soft rock.
So now, cliffs of hard rock jut out, forming a **headland**.

3 Here the softer rock has been eroded away, leaving a **bay**.

4 Another headland. Here you can see a **cave**, an **arch** and a **stack**.

cave
arch
stack

2 At the base of these cliffs is a **wave-cut platform**.

How a wave-cut platform forms

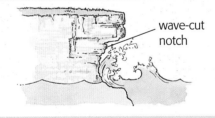
wave-cut notch

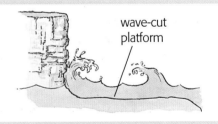
wave-cut platform

1 The waves carve **wave-cut notches** into cliffs at a headland. These get deeper and deeper …

2 … until, one day, the rock above them collapses. The sea carries the debris away.

3 The process continues non-stop. Slowly the cliffs retreat, leaving a **wave-cut platform** behind.

How caves, arches and stacks form

cave

arch

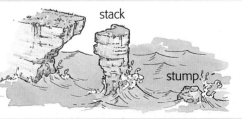
stack
stump

1 The sea attacks cracks in the cliff at a headland. The cracks grow larger – and form a **cave**.

2 The cave gets eroded all the way through. It turns into an **arch**. Then one day …

3 … the arch collapses, leaving a **stack**. In time, the waves erode the stack to a **stump**.

6 Some is deposited in sheltered areas like this one, forming a **beach**.

7 Here the coast bends to form a bay with calmer water, which interrupts the longshore drift …

10 Silt and mud may build up in this sheltered area. It becomes a **salt marsh**.

salt marsh

9 The end of the spit is curved by the waves.

spit

5 Eroded material is carried along the coast by longshore drift.

8 … so sand and shingle are deposited here, in the sea. They build up a **spit**.

Your turn

1

Landform	Created by ...	
	erosion	deposition
headland		

Make a table like the one started here. Write in the names of all the landforms you met in this unit. Then put a ✓ to show how each was formed.

2 Make a larger sketch of the landforms in photo A.
   a On your sketch, label:
      a wave-cut notch   an arch   a stump
   b Explain how the arch was formed.
   c Draw a dotted line to show where there was once another arch.
   d What will happen to the stump over time?

3 Photo B shows the spit at Dawlish Warren in Devon.
   a Make a sketch of the spit. Don't forget to show and label the groynes, and salt marsh areas.
   b From which direction does the prevailing wind blow? How did you decide? Mark the direction on your sketch.

4

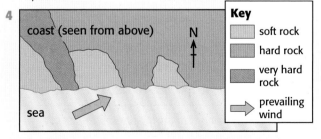

coast (seen from above)   N

sea

Key
soft rock
hard rock
very hard rock
prevailing wind

This shows some coast before erosion. Make a larger drawing to show how it may look 10 000 years from now. Label any landforms, and annotate (add notes to) your drawing to explain what has happened.

A

B

N

Along the East Lothian coast

In this unit you will explore one stretch of Scotland's coast, using an OS map.

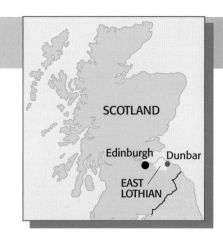

SCOTLAND

Edinburgh • Dunbar

EAST
LOTHIAN

Be a coastline detective!

Scotland has a very exciting coast. The OS map opposite shows part of the East Lothian coast, east of Edinburgh. Study it. Then try these questions. (The key on page 126 will help.)

Your turn

1 Look at photo **A** below the OS map on page 105.
   a What type of landform does it show?
   b Find the landform on the OS map, and give a 4-figure grid reference for this part of it.
   c What is the land made of, on this landform?
   d In which direction does the prevailing wind blow, on this section of the coast? What is your evidence?
   e Name the sea area shown in the right of the photo.
   f A river joins the sea at the tip of the landform. Which river?

2 Now look at photo **B** below the OS map.
   a Find this same area on the OS map. Which square is most of it in?
   b Look at the house marked with the yellow dot on the photo. See if you can find it on the map, and give its 6-figure grid reference.

3 The map below shows the types of rock in this area.
   a What kind of rock are the Long Craigs (6679)?
   b What can you say about the rock in the Hedderwick Hill area (6478 and 6479)?
   c Of the three types of rock shown on the map, which one erodes the most easily? Explain your choice.
   d The landform in photo A is not shown on this map. See if you can suggest a reason.

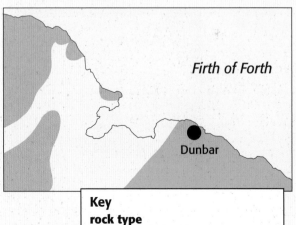

Firth of Forth

Dunbar

Key
rock type
   old red sandstone
   igneous rock (from volcanoes)
   mix of mudstone, siltstone and sandstone

4 Photo **C**, above, shows the ruins of Dunbar Castle. Mary Queen of Scots took refuge here in 1566.
   a Look for these castle ruins, in photo B.
   b Now find them on the OS map, and see if you can give a six-figure grid reference.
   c Why do you think this site was chosen, for a castle?
   d Where was the photographer standing, for this shot?
     i 681795   ii 674795   iii 680793

5 It is May, and the weather is fine. You have to plan a *long* walk (at least 12 km) for a group of geography students from Glasgow. These are the rules:

   ◆ Start at the car park in square 6678.
   ◆ Show a variety of landforms, and anything else the group may find interesting.
   ◆ Include a beach walk (even if only a short one).
   ◆ Use footpaths where available.
   ◆ Try to avoid retracing your steps, where possible.
   ◆ Finish at the school at 669786, for tea.

   a Draw a sketch map for your planned route, showing the main features you will see, or visit. Label them.
   b Mark any places where the walk may be dangerous. Add a note to say why.
   c And finally, make a list of what to take with you.

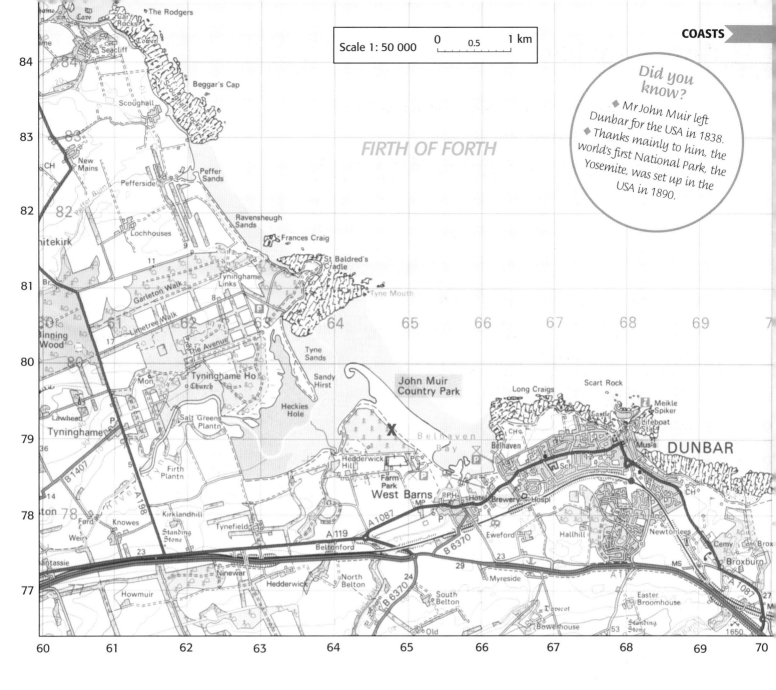

Scale 1: 50 000

0   0.5   1 km

FIRTH OF FORTH

In this unit you will learn why land use in coastal areas needs to be managed.

We do love to be beside the seaside!

People love the coast. But there's only a limited amount of it. If we all did as we pleased there, it would be chaotic.

So the coast has to be **managed**, in a **sustainable** way. That means people have to agree on the best way to use it, that will not spoil it, and then put the plan into action.

Who manages land use in our coastal areas?

The coast, like the rest of the UK, is managed mostly by **local councils**. These are made up of local people. (When you are 18 you can vote for your local council.)

Suppose you want to build a new golf course or hotel along the coast. This is what to do:

> *Did you know?*
> ◆ You can own land along the coast – but not under the sea.
> ◆ The sea bed, and land below high tide, belong to the Crown.

COUNCIL NOTICE
Proposal for new development

CLOSING DATE
FOR OBJECTIONS
14th APRIL.

| Send your plan to the local council, and ask for planning permission. | → | The council may like the plan. But it still has to send out notices to ask if anyone objects. | → | A **public inquiry** may be held, where people come to state their objections. | → | An inspector will study the objections, and decide if the plan can go ahead. |

In Scotland, the inspectors are called **reporters**.
Sometimes, for big projects, the government (or Scottish Executive) gets involved. It can over-rule the council and turn down a plan, or agree to it.

Your turn

1

Work	Leisure
farming	walking

Make a table like this to show how the coast around the UK is used. The drawing on page 106 will help.

2 A **conflict grid** is started below, for the drawing on page 106. It's a way to show where conflicts arise.

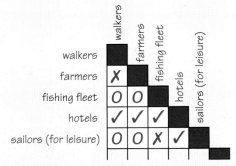

a The **✗** shows that farmers and walkers may come into conflict with each other. Suggest a reason why.

b The **✓** shows that the hotels and fishing fleet may benefit each other. Explain why.

c The **O** shows that sailors and walkers do not affect each other. Why not?

3 a Draw your own grid for the people in the drawing. (Your table for question **1** will help.)

b Fill in a ✓, ✗ or O in each empty square.

c For each conflict (✗), suggest a way to solve the problem.

4 Now turn to the OS map on page 105.
Dunbar is not as busy as the place in the drawing – but there is still plenty going on.
What leisure activities are there for visitors, in the map area? Look for clues, and give four-figure grid references.

5 Dream Developments are **developers**. They want to build a leisure complex at Dunbar.
You can see a photo of the proposed site, and a drawing of the complex, below. The site is also marked with an **X** on the OS map on page 105.

a In which direction was the camera pointing, for the photo below?

b What are **developers**? (Glossary?)

c The site is a **greenfield site**. See if you can guess what that means. Then have a look in the glossary.

6 You work for Dream Developments. Using the OS map to help you, draw a sketch to suggest where a road into the complex could be built.

7 You are the head of Dream Developments. Write a letter to the East Lothian council to say how your plan will help the area. For example you could mention:
◆ how good you think the complex will look
◆ how it will help tourism
◆ how you can provide work for local people.

8 There will be a public enquiry about this proposal. You will attend.

a First, study the OS map. Do you think this site is a wise choice for any building? What might the drawbacks be?

b List any good points about the proposal.

c Now list negative points. For example how might the complex affect wildlife? the scenery? traffic?

d So, do you think the leisure complex should go ahead? Write a short speech for the public enquiry, stating your opinion. Give your main reasons (no more than three).

9 The proposal is rejected. But Dream Developments wants to try again, with a **brownfield site** in Dunbar. Suggest a site that may be suitable, and give its grid reference.

gyms and dance studios

swimming pools, saunas, steam rooms

DUNBAR DREAM LEISURE

health and beauty treatments

cafe, juice bar, shop

watersports centre

SAIL CENTRE

In this unit you'll see how erosion by the waves is causing big problems in one English coastal village.

Life on the brink

George and Jeanne Scott had planned to enjoy their retirement in their home by the sea, in Happisburgh in Norfolk. (Pronounce it *Haisbro*!)

But their plans have changed. On Monday the waves claimed their garden. Now their porch is teetering on the edge of the cliff. They have moved into the back bedroom, just in case. But they know it won't be long before the whole house falls into the sea.

They won't sleep much tonight. Outside, the storm is still raging. Waves crash over the roof, and slam against the windows, and make the whole house shake.

'We don't like to make a fuss,' said Mrs Scott, 'but we are upset about losing our home. We can't afford another, because we won't get compensation for this one. But the council has found us a bungalow to rent.'

Meanwhile their neighbours watch the storm nervously. If nobody helps Happisburgh to fight erosion, how long can it hang on?

Adapted from a newspaper article, 22 February 1996

▲ *The Scotts' home (●). Going, going ...*

Why is erosion so severe at Happisburgh?

1 The main problem is that the cliffs are soft – sand on top and clay below.

2 Rain soaks into the cliffs and helps to weaken them. (This is one form of **weathering**.) The more rain they hold, the weaker they get.

3 Meanwhile, the waves erode the cliffs from below. In calm weather erosion will be slower ...

4 ... but when there's a storm, big waves batter the cliffs, and big chunks of them collapse.

5 These wooden barriers (or **revetments**) were meant to slow down erosion, by making the waves break early. But they were destroyed in a past storm.

groyne

Your turn

1 What part did each play in the loss of the Scotts' home to the sea?
   a the material the cliffs were made of
   b rain
   c strong north winds blowing down the North Sea

2 Now look at the aerial photos of Happisburgh below, and the little OS map on the right.
   a What are all the white objects near the top of each photo? (The OS map will help.)
   b In which compass direction was the camera pointing?
   c Look at the wooden barriers on both photos.
      i What are the ones at right angles to the cliffs called? What is their job?
      ii What are the ones parallel to the cliffs called? What is their job?
      iii The second photo shows another type of barrier, made of rocks. What is it called? Check page 110!

3 a Now list all the changes you notice for the coast in the photos, between 1996 and 2004.
   b From the photos, do you think the barriers:
      i prevented erosion? ii slowed it down?

4 Even where there are barriers, the cliffs at Happisburgh are eroding at a rate of about 2 m a year. Where there are no barriers, the rate is about 8 m a year.

   Suppose the barriers remain as they are in the second photo below. Based on this OS map, about how long will it be before the sea reaches:
   a the church?
   b the lighthouse?
   (The photos don't show the lighthouse.)

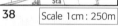

Scale 1cm : 250m

▲ *Happisburgh in 1996, over eight months after the Scotts lost their home. (It was around ● .)*

▲ *Happisburgh in 2004. Homes are still disappearing, at a rate of about one a year.*

The war against erosion

In this unit you'll find out where erosion is a problem on the UK coast, and what we can do about it.

It's not just Happisburgh!

In the last unit you saw that erosion is a big problem in Happisburgh (say *Haisbro*). But it is not alone.

This map shows the main stretches of the UK coastline where erosion is a major problem. In these places the sea is nibbling away at land and homes, causing people a great deal of worry.

Some erosion goes on everywhere, of course. But where it is very slow, and does not affect settlements, it is not a problem.

Rock types in the UK

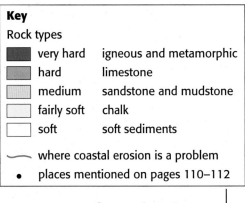

Key

Rock types

▓	very hard	igneous and metamorphic
▒	hard	limestone
░	medium	sandstone and mudstone
□	fairly soft	chalk
□	soft	soft sediments

⌒ where coastal erosion is a problem

• places mentioned on pages 110–112

• Mappleton

• Happisburgh

• Highcliffe

*Courtesy of Catherine Poulton,
British Geological Survey*

So how can we stop coastal erosion?

Coastal erosion is caused by the waves, and helped by weathering. So here are ways to stop or at least reduce it.

You could build **sea walls** like this one, to stop the waves reaching valuable land …

… or a barrier of large rocks (**rock armour**) to soak up their energy. Less energy means less erosion.

You could even build the barrier out at sea, to make the waves break earlier, away from the beach.

You could build **groynes** to stop sand being carried away. The sand in turn protects the land behind.

So you could build up a beach by adding more sand or shingle. This is called **beach replenishment**.

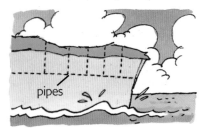

Where cliffs soak up the rain, you could put pipes in to drain them. This will slow down weathering.

How Mappleton was saved

The first photo below shows the village of Mappleton, on the north east coast of England, in 1990. (Look on the map on page 110.) It's about to slide into the sea.

But the people fought hard for a grant to build coastal defences. The second photo shows the defences in place. They cost over £2 million.

Did you know?
◆ Over the centuries, dozens of villages on the coast around Mappleton have been lost to the sea, through erosion.

▲ *Mappleton in 1990 – just hanging on.*

▲ *Mappleton in 1992, after its new coastal defences were built.*

Your turn

1 Look at the map on page 110.
   a Where is most of:
      i the very hard rock? ii the soft rock?
   b Does the map show a link between rock type and erosion? Describe what you notice.
   c Where on the coast is erosion a problem? Give your answer as a paragraph. Mention Scotland, Wales and Northern Ireland in it.

2 Look at the photo of Mappleton above, after its coastal defences were built.
   a What was done: at **A**? at **B**? at **C**? Explain how each will help to prevent erosion.
   b Look again at **C**. Has the structure here helped to prevent erosion? Explain your answer.
   c They could have continued the defences from **C** to **D**, or even further. But they stopped at **C**.
      i Why do you think they stopped? (Hint: land use.)
      ii What is likely to happen, as a result?

3 Now look back at the second photo of Happisburgh, on page 109. You live in one of the houses with the red roofs, near the sea. And you are getting very worried about erosion.
   a Write a letter to the local newspaper saying why you are worried, and what you think the local council should do.
   b Say how much you think the council might have to spend. The list below *might* help, depending on your suggestions.

Cost of coastal defences

Defence	Costs about
Sea wall	£5000 per metre
Rock armour	£2500 per metre
Wooden revetment	£1500 per metre
Typical rock groyne	£125 000
Typical wooden groyne	£100 000
Beach nourishment	£10 per cubic metre

Managing the defence of the coast

In this unit you'll find out what the problems are, in defending the coast against erosion – and who makes the decisions, and what the strategy is.

The problems with fighting erosion

In many places around the coast, erosion is threatening land and homes. So why don't they just build defences everywhere? It's not that simple!

First, coastal defences cost a lot. Rock armour like this costs about £2500 per metre. Sea walls cost about £5000 per metre.

And they don't last forever. Look at these revetments at Happisburgh, destroyed in a storm. So you just have to keep on spending.

There's another big problem: global warming. It is causing sea levels to rise – and causing more storms too.

That means we'll get bigger and stronger waves – so we'll need bigger and stronger defences to cope with them.

Finally, preventing erosion in one place can make it worse in others. These groynes at Highcliffe (see the map on page 110) may be …

… speeding up erosion at Naish Farm, nearby. (But you'd need to measure erosion before and after building groynes, to prove it.)

So who decides?

There are many towns and cities on or near near the UK coast. Over 15% of the population live within a few km of it. So erosion is a big headache for the government.

What happens is this:

- The government sets out a strategy for coastal defence.
- Along the coast, local councils make decisions based on the strategy.
- Some of the money for defences comes from the government. The local councils come up with the rest.

Did you know?
- Millions of tonnes of sand and gravel are dredged from the sea bed each year, for new buildings and roads.
- Some people think this is making coastal erosion worse.

What's the strategy ?

The strategy is to defend the coast in a **sustainable** way. That means build defences only where it makes sense, and where they won't do harm. These are the key ideas:

◆ If land and houses are worth less than the defences will cost, do not defend them.

◆ Think about the effect of defences on other places, and on wildlife.

◆ When planning land use along the coast in future, always keep erosion in mind.

So where does this leave Happisburgh ?

As you saw in Unit 7.6, more of Happisburgh (say *Haisbro*) will slip into the sea. So far, plans for new defences have been rejected, because they will cost more than the land and houses are worth. But the local people say it's not fair. They are still fighting their case.

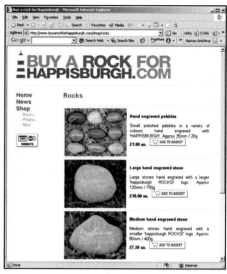

▲ *Raising money to save Happisburgh.*

Your turn

1 Make a list of the problems we face, in defending the coast against erosion. Give them in order, with what you think is the most serious one first.

2 Do you agree with this person? Explain.

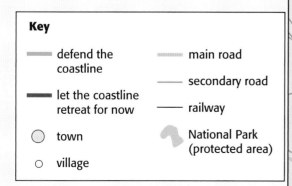

3 The map on the right shows the local council's plans for fighting erosion on the north coast of Norfolk (where Happisburgh is).

 a Some of the coastline will not be defended. What do you think is the main reason?

 b Name two villages that won't be defended, at least for the present.

4 a The council plans to keep on defending Cromer. Using clues from the map, suggest a reason. Say which clues you used.

 b It plans to protect Sea Palling, which has fewer than 600 people. See if you can find a reason for this, from the map.

 c It does not plan to protect Winterton for now. What questions would you ask about Winterton, to understand why?

5 You live in Happisburgh, near the cliffs. (See the photos on page 109.) You want to sell your house and move away. But no one will buy it, because of the council's plans. So what will you do? Come up with a plan of action.

Key

═══	defend the coastline	▪▪▪▪ main road
═══	let the coastline retreat for now	─── secondary road
◯	town	─── railway
○	village	🌲 National Park (protected area)

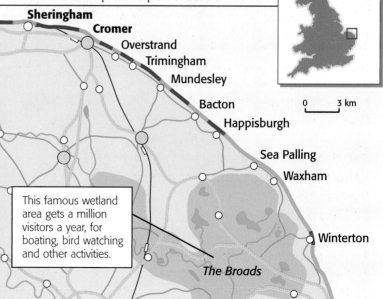

This famous wetland area gets a million visitors a year, for boating, bird watching and other activities.

Sheringham · Cromer · Overstrand · Trimingham · Mundesley · Bacton · Happisburgh · Sea Palling · Waxham · Winterton · *The Broads*

0   3 km

The big picture

Geography is brilliant – it even covers sport! This chapter takes football as an example. These are the big ideas behind the chapter:

◆ Football links people and places all around the world.

◆ It's fun – but it's also big business, and lots of people depend on it for a living (not just the players).

◆ Some earn a fortune from it. But people in poorer countries who make the kit get paid very little.

◆ A football stadium can have a big impact on its surroundings.

These ideas apply to many other sports too.

Your goals for this chapter

By the end of this chapter you should be able to answer these questions:

◆ In what ways does football link people and places around the world?

◆ Are the UK's most successful teams in the biggest towns and cities? If so, why is this?

◆ What do these terms mean?

   economic activity   *primary sector*   *secondary sector*   *tertiary sector*

◆ What kinds of jobs are linked to football?

◆ Why is football described as big business?

◆ What kind of impact does a stadium have on an area?

◆ When clubs move stadiums, who gains and who may lose out?

◆ Why is so much of the sports kit sold here made in poorer countries?

And then …

When you finish the chapter, come back to this page and see if you have met your goals!

Did you know?

◆ Around 200 BC in China, 'football' meant kicking a leather ball, filled with hair and feathers, through an opening less than 50 cm wide.

Did you know?

◆ In 1314 the Mayor of London banned football in the city, because it caused such a rumpus.

◆ People caught playing it could be sent to prison.

Did you know?

◆ Football is now the top sport played by girls and women in the UK.

Your chapter starter

Football is just geography in action!

Look at the photo on page 114.

The ball was made in Pakistan, and the boots in India. The match may be wached on TV in Nigeria, and Japan, and many other countries.

What other links to geography can you find in the photo?
Come up with as many as you can.

Come on my son!

Exploring success in football

In this unit you'll explore some reasons why some teams – and some countries – are more successful at football than others.

The football winners

▲ *World Cup winners, 2006: Italy.*

▲ *Olympic Football champions, 2004: USA.*

Every club, and every country, likes to win at football.

So why do some do better than others? Is it just about talent? Or the size of a place? Or is it all down to money? It's up to you to explore!

Your turn

First, get warmed up

1 Your task is to match each dot on the map to the correct football club, from the list below.

> Sheffield Wednesday
> Newcastle United
> Manchester United
> Cardiff City
> Liverpool
> Brighton
> Arsenal
> Blackpool
> Hull City
> Aberdeen

Write your answer like this: **A** = _____
(And no foul play or you'll be sent off!)

2 Football teams are in different **leagues**, depending on how good they are. Name as many leagues for England and Wales as you can, in order, best first.

Is success linked to the size of a place?

3 Do bigger cities tend to have better football teams? It's time to find out. The first table on page 117 shows 24 towns and cities in England and Wales (outside London) with teams in the top four leagues.

a Which is the *largest* city or town in the list *without* a team in the Premier League?

b Which is the *smallest* city or town *with* a team in the Premier League?

4 a Now make a large copy of the scattergraph started below. (Use graph paper if you can. Use a full page, turned sideways.) Put in all the lines shown here.

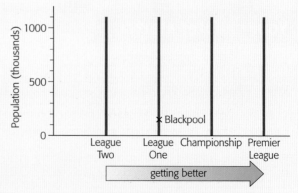

UK city or town	Population (thousands)	Team(s)	League (2006–07)
Birmingham	977	Aston Villa	Premier
		Birmingham City	Championship
Blackpool	142	Blackpool	One
Bristol	421	Bristol City	One
Darlington	98	Darlington	Two
Derby	289	Derby County	Championship
Huddersfield	146	Huddersfield Town	One
Ipswich	117	Ipswich Town	Championship
Leicester	280	Leicester City	Championship
Liverpool	439	Liverpool	Premier
		Everton	Premier
Luton	184	Luton Town	Championship
Macclesfield	150	Macclesfield Town	Two
Manchester	393	Manchester United	Premier
		Manchester City	Premier
Newcastle	276	Newcastle United	Premier
Northampton	194	Northampton Town	One
Oldham	217	Oldham Athletic	One
Peterborough	156	Peterborough United	Two
Reading	233	Reading	Premier
Sheffield	513	Sheffield United	Premier
		Sheffield Wednesday	Championship
Shrewsbury	100	Shrewsbury Town	Two
Southampton	217	Southampton	Championship
Southend	160	Southend United	Championship
Swindon	180	Swindon Town	Two
Walsall	253	Walsall	Two
Wolverhampton	234	Wolverhampton Wanderers	Championship

b Complete your graph for all 24 places in the table. Then make up a title for it.

c Look at your scattergraph. Does it show a link between the population of places and the success of their teams? Describe any *overall* trend you can see.

d Try to think up reasons to explain this trend.

5 a Now draw a larger copy of this flowchart.

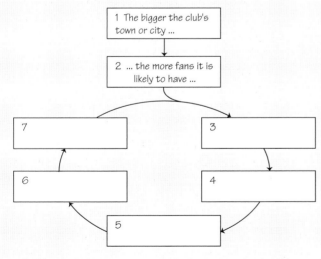

```
1 The bigger the club's
  town or city ...
        |
        v
2 ... the more fans it is
  likely to have ...
     /          \
    /            \
  [7]            [3]
   ^              |
   |              v
  [6]            [4]
    \            /
     \          /
        [5]
```

b Write in the five part-sentences below in the right boxes, to complete the flowchart. (One per box.)

...so then it can buy in more good players...

...so it can sell more match tickets...

...so it will win more matches...

...so it will get more fans...

...which means it will make more money...

c Look at your completed flowchart for b. Does it help to explain the pattern you found in 4?

d Do you agree with the logic in your flowchart? Give it a mark out of 10.

Are poorer countries less successful at football?

6 '*Poorer countries are not as successful as richer countries, at football!*'
Do you agree? Answer *Yes*, *No* or *Not sure*.

7 This table shows the 2006 world football rankings for some countries, and the average wealth per person in these countries (in US dollars).

Country/ nation	FIFA ranking in 2006	Average wealth per person (in US$)
Argentina	3	12 000
Brazil	1	8000
Croatia	24	11 000
France	2	28 000
Germany	8	28 000
Ghana	23	2200
Italy	5	27 000
Japan	47	28 000
Kenya	127	1000
Mali	60	1000
Morocco	41	4000
Niger	167	800
Nigeria	11	1000
Scotland	34	27 000
United States	29	38 000

a In which one of these countries are people richest, on average? In which are they poorest?

b Now draw a scattergraph for the data in the table. You will need *long* axes. Label them as started here:

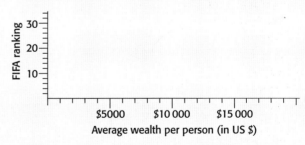

c Study your scattergraph. Then answer question 6 again – and this time give your evidence.

d Can you suggest anything further you could do, to check for links between wealth and success in football? (The world has over 200 countries!)

8 Look again at the table above. Use it to explain why:
a some top Brazilian players have joined English teams.
b players from England don't join Brazilian teams.

Earning a living from football

In this unit you'll learn about jobs linked to football – and a way to classify them.

Jobs in a football club

You don't have to play football to get a job in a football club! Look at these:

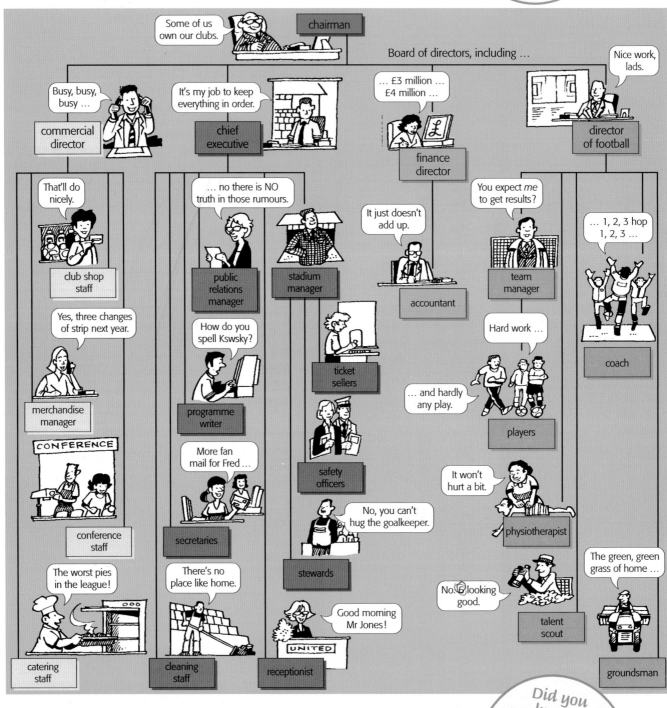

Other jobs that depend on football

Hundreds of other jobs *outside* the clubs also depend on football. Like these:

- sewing football strip (the kit the players wear)
- writing about football for a newspaper
- running the football pools.

Your turn

1 Look at the drawing of the football club on page 118.
   a Who is in charge of the players?
     See if you can name one real person with this job.
   b What do the catering staff do?
   c What does a physiotherapist do?
   d What does the groundsman do?
   e Explain what a board of directors is, in your
     own words.

2 *Economic activity* means work you get paid for.
  It can be divided into four kinds or **sectors**:

primary – you collect
things from the Earth.
Farming, fishing, mining.

secondary – you make or
manufacture things. Like
shoes, chairs, paint.

tertiary – you provide
services. Like teach, or
look after sick people.

quaternary – you do
hi-tech work. Like develop
new drugs to cure disease.

   Now look again at the jobs in the football club.
   a Are any of them in the quaternary sector?
   b Do any belong to the primary or secondary sectors?
     (Did you have any problem deciding? If so, why?)
   c Overall, what can you say about jobs in a football club?

3 a Now draw a large spider map to show jobs *outside*
     the club that are linked to football. Give as many as
     you can. You could start like this:

   football writer

   Jobs that are linked to
   football (outside the club)

   strip designer

   b On your spider map, underline any primary sector
     jobs in one colour, secondary in another, and so on.
     Add a key to explain the colours.

4 This is the story of replica football strip:

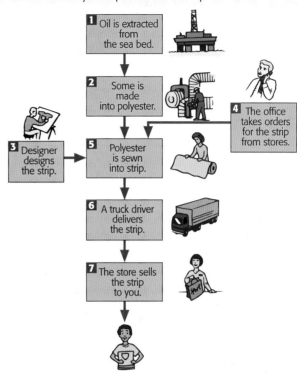

1 Oil is extracted
  from
  the sea bed.

2 Some is
  made
  into polyester.

3 Designer
  designs
  the strip.

4 The office
  takes orders
  for the strip
  from stores.

5 Polyester
  is sewn
  into strip.

6 A truck driver
  delivers
  the strip.

7 The store sells
  the strip
  to you.

   a Make your own copy of the flowchart.
     (Leave out the drawings!)
   b Now underline any primary activities in one
     colour, secondary in another colour, and so on.
   c Add a key to show what the colours mean.

5 Lots of people earn a living from football – but some
  earn more than others! This shows pay in one club:

Job	Pay per year
cleaner	£10 000
catering manager	£36 000
coach	£85 000
stadium manager	£60 000
player	£250 000
team manager	£100 000
secretary	£24 000

   a Draw a bar chart to show this data.
     (Turn your graph paper sideways?)
     Show the pay in order, starting with the largest.
   b The player earns ___ times as much as the
     cleaner. What's the missing number?
   c Do you think he works ___ times as hard as
     the cleaner?
   d Do you think this big difference in pay is fair?

The football business

In this unit you'll learn how the big football clubs earn money – and how good players and stadiums help.

It's big business

Football is not just a game – it is big business. The top clubs earn, and spend, millions of pounds a year. These photos give clues about how they earn money. (You will have to match the numbers to words later.)

Now look at the list on the right. It shows how clubs spend money. Some get into trouble because they spend more than they earn!

How clubs spend money
- paying the players
- paying other staff
- buying new players
- improving stadiums
- hosting matches
- going to away matches
- training youth teams
- working with schools

And not just for the clubs

It's not just the big football clubs that make money from football.

Local shops, cafes, pubs and restaurants are all busier than usual on match days.

They'll be ever so hungry ▶
and thirsty after this.

Your turn

How a big football club makes money

		Could the club earn more from this by ...	
	Way of making money	having better players?	moving to a bigger, better stadium?
1	selling match tickets		yes
2			

1 These are ways a big football club makes money:
   - selling match tickets
   - catering (bars and restaurants)
   - selling merchandise (strip, scarves, and so on)
   - TV fees (for matches shown on TV)
   - renting out rooms for conferences
   - renting out private viewing boxes
   - sponsorship

   You have to match them to the numbers 1–7 in the photos on page 120. Here is what to do.

   a Make a table with headings like the one above. Extend it to show rows numbered 1–7.

   b Write the correct items in column 2, to match the photo numbers. (Pick from the list above.)

   c Do you think a club will sell more tickets if it has better players? Write *yes* or *no* in row 1, column 3.

   d Fill in column 3 for all the other rows.

   e Now decide if moving stadiums will affect what the club can earn for each item, and fill in the last column.

2 Draw a spider map to show who else gains when a football club is successful. You could start like this:

3 Like every business, football clubs need to make money. Many buy players from all over the world, to help them do that. This will show how it works:

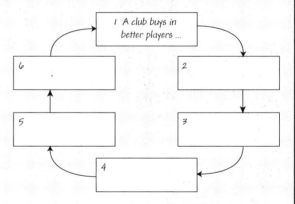

Make a larger copy of the flowchart.
Then write these in the correct boxes ...

   ... so it can afford more of the world's top players.

   ... which means it sells more tickets and more merchandise.

   So the club gets richer and richer...

   ... so it wins more and more matches...

   This also means it makes more money from TV and sponsorship.

4 And back to stadiums again. Around the UK, many clubs have moved to new stadiums, or are thinking about it. Using your table for 1 to help you, write a paragraph to explain why.

In this unit you will explore Arsenal's move in 2006 to its new stadium – and the impact of the move.

It's all go for the Gunners!

In 1913, Arsenal played its first game at Highbury. In 2006, 93 years later, it played its first game at its stunning new home in Ashburton Grove.

'We were sad to leave Highbury,' said manager Arsene Wenger. 'But it held only 38 500 people. The new stadium holds 60 000. Our fans are happy to see more tickets on sale. This is the start a new era for the club.'

Not just a stadium

The cost of the project: a staggering £390 million! But not all just for the stadium. The redevelopment at Ashburton Grove includes:

- over 2000 new homes
- space for shops and other businesses
- a new sports and community centre for the local people
- 2 new gyms
- 4 community health centres.

But it has not all been plain sailing. Arsenal had problems raising the money for the scheme, and now has big debts. And many local people objected to Arsenal's plans. Two even went to the High Court to fight them – but lost.

Letters to the editor

Dear Sir

So Arsenal have moved in. And now we have 60 000 fans to cope with.

Every match day, 17 local roads are closed off. What a pain! And for some roads you need to show a resident's permit – to get into your own road – before a match starts! Can you believe that?

With the crowds of fans, it's impossible to use the tube or buses around match times. And then there's the noise. And the litter.

No wonder I shut myself in a darkened room on match days.

Yours in disgust

Pete Phillips

Your turn

1 What was the main reason for Arsenal's move?

2 When the club first talked about moving, the fans made lots of suggestions. Here are two:

Give reasons why the club said no to each.

3 a Make a table with headings like the one below.

Finding a new site for a football stadium	
Things to think about	Score for Ashburton Grove
Large enough?	
Close to public transport?	
Near our fans?	

b In the first column, list more things you'd think about, if you had to find a new site for a stadium.

c In the second column, give Ashburton Grove a score for each. (0 = poor, 5 = excellent.)

4 Look at the aerial photo on page 123. In which direction was the camera pointing?

5 The local council forced Arsenal to build some things to help the local people, in return for permission to use the site. See if you can identify them from the list above.

6 a Make a large table like the one started below. You could use a new page, turned sideways.

The impact of the Ashburton Grove redevelopment			
on Arsenal FC		on the local people	
positive	negative	positive	negative
....	....	....	....

b Now complete the table. Under *positive* write the benefits. Under *negative* write the bad points. Try to think of everything. For example what will the effect be on local traffic? On the tube stations?

c Overall:

i has Arsenal FC gained more than it lost?

ii have the local people gained more than they lost?

Arsenal's home area

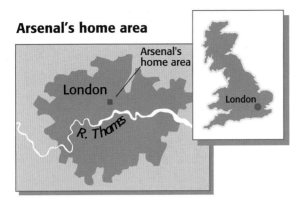

London

R. Thames

Arsenal's home area

London

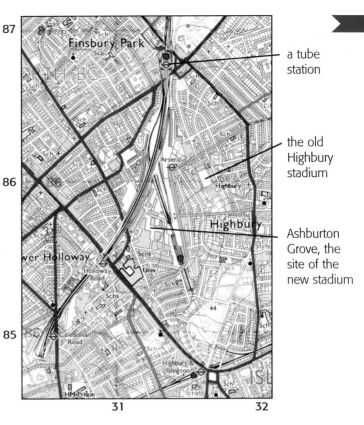

a tube station

the old Highbury stadium

Ashburton Grove, the site of the new stadium

Scale 1 cm: 250 m

▲ *An OS map (2002) showing the sites of the old and new stadiums. They are just a short walk apart.*

The Highbury stands are being turned into flats. The pitch will be planted with trees.

Some of this site was waste ground – but not all. Over 60 businesses had to move, to make way for the new stadium.

◀ *The new stadium being built at Ashburton Grove, in 2004. Look at the old Highbury stadium in the background.*

▲ *Fans enjoying the view from the restaurant.*

◀*The new stadium at Ashburton Grove, in 2006. Why does it say Emirates?*

Who are the losers?

In this unit you'll learn how some 'football' workers are paid very unfairly.

Football skills

This player earned around £1500 today for kicking this ball. (He scored a goal, with great skill.)

The football is made of rubber and synthetic leather. It is top quality. It could cost £65 in the shops.

It was sewn by hand, with great skill, by Omar, aged 14. It took him 3 hours. He got paid 65p.

Omar lives on the outskirts of Sialkot in Pakistan.

In that city, and the villages around it, they make 75% of the world's hand-stitched footballs. They produce an amazing 35 million footballs a year.

A vicious circle

Why is Omar paid so little? This is what happens:

This British company supplies footballs. It gets them made …

… and then sells them to clubs and sports shops at a profit.

We must make more profit …

The less it pays for the footballs the more profit it will make …

… so it searches the world for a factory to make them cheaply.

The footballs are shipped to the UK. They have been well made. The British company is happy.

But what can we do?

They can't leave because they need the work. If they don't have jobs they will starve.

That's the best I can offer.

He also wants to make as much profit as he can. So he pays his workers very little.

That's the best I can offer.

This factory owner in Sialkot wants the work – but if he charges too much he won't get it.

It's not just British companies. It happens in all the richer countries.
They get things made in poorer countries where wages are lower.
Not just footballs, but football strip, and boots, and other sports items.
You will find out more about this later in your course.

Omar's story

I have been sewing footballs since I was 8.

I don't like it much. But I have to do it, because my dad died and we need the money. My mum used to sew too but now she has trouble with her eyes. So I have to support my family.

I work in a stitching centre. I start at 7 in the morning and often work till 8 in the evening. I do 4 footballs a day – so I earn £2.60 a day. But they can throw me out any time. I don't know what I will do if that happens.

I get tired of sewing all day. My shoulders get stiff. My eyes get sore. My fingers are all cut. I would love to go to school instead – but no chance!

I saw a World Cup match on the TV at my uncle's house. The football could have been one I sewed. But nobody at the match knew about me!

■ Omar at work.

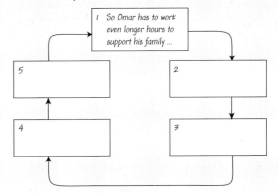

Your turn

1 A certain Premier League footballer earns £15 000 a week. (The really big stars earn a lot more.) How long would Omar have to work to earn that much?

2 Suppose you buy a football for £50, made in Sialkot. Where does the money go? It could go like this:

	£
The shop where you bought it	10.00
The British supplier	31.00
Shipping and transport companies	1.50
The Sialkot factory owner	5.00
The company that supplied the materials for the football	1.50
The stitcher	0.50
Other factory costs (lighting etc)	0.50
Total	**£50.00**

What percentage of the money does the factory owner get? You can work it out like this:

$$\frac{\text{factory owner's share}}{\text{total amount}} \times 100\%$$

$$= \frac{£5}{£50} \times 100 = 10\%$$

a Now work out the percentages for the others in the list.

b Draw a pie chart to show how the money is shared.

c Who gets: the largest share? the smallest?

3 Look at the 'vicious circle' on page 124. What might happen if:

a the stitchers went on strike?

b the factory manager tried to charge the British company more?

c the British company charged the shops more?

d everyone refused to use footballs made in Pakistan?

e someone invented a machine that could sew footballs perfectly?

4 In some ways, Omar's life is also a vicious circle.

Make a larger copy of the drawing above, Then write the following in the correct boxes.

... but every year food and clothes cost a little more ...

... so he can't get a better-paid job ...

... so he has even less chance to go to school ...

... so he can't learn new skills (like reading and writing) ...

5 How would you make life less unfair for the stitchers? Give your answer in not less than 150 words.

Ordnance Survey symbols

ROADS AND PATHS

M 1 or A 6(M)	Motorway
A 35	Dual carriageway
A 31(T) or A 35	Trunk or main road
B 3074	Secondary road
	Road generally more than 4 m wide
	Road generally less than 4 m wide
	Other road, drive or track, fenced and unfenced
– – – – – – –	Path

PUBLIC RIGHTS OF WAY

(Not applicable to Scotland)

1:25 000	1:50 000	
....	....	Footpath
— — —	– · – · –	Road used as a public footpath
+–+–+–+	– – – –	Bridleway
·–·–·–·	–+–+–+–·–	Byway open to all traffic

RAILWAYS

	Multiple track
	Single track
	Narrow gauge/Light rapid transit system
	Road over; road under; level crossing
	Cutting; tunnel; embankment
	Station, open to passengers; siding

BOUNDARIES

+ — + — +	National
+ · + · + · +	District
— · — · —	County, Unitary Authority, Metropolitan District or London Borough
	National Park

HEIGHTS/ROCK FEATURES

Contour lines ——50——

Spot height to the nearest metre above sea level:

52 found by ground survey
119 found by air survey

outcrop   cliff   scree

ABBREVIATIONS

P	Post office	PC	Public convenience (rural areas)
PH	Public house	TH	Town Hall, Guildhall or equivalent
MS	Milestone	Sch	School
MP	Milepost	Coll	College
CH	Clubhouse	Mus	Museum
CG	Coastguard	Cemy	Cemetery
Fm	Farm		

ANTIQUITIES

VILLA	Roman	✕	Battlefield (with date)
Castle	Non-Roman	☆	Tumulus

LAND FEATURES

	Buildings
	Public building
	Bus or coach station
Place of Worship	with tower / with spire, minaret or dome / without such additions
°	Chimney or tower
	Glass structure
Ⓗ	Heliport
△	Triangulation pillar
	Mast
	Wind pump / wind generator
	Windmill
+	Graticule intersection
	Cutting, embankment
	Quarry
	Spoil heap, refuse tip or dump
	Coniferous wood
	Non-coniferous wood
	Mixed wood
	Orchard
	Park or ornamental ground
	Forestry Commission access land
	National Trust – always open
	National Trust, limited access, observe local signs
	National Trust for Scotland

TOURIST INFORMATION

P	Parking
V	Visitor centre
i	Information centre
☏	Telephone
	Camp site/Caravan site
	Golf course or links
	Viewpoint
PC	Public convenience
✕	Picnic site
	Pub/s
	Cathedral/Abbey
	Museum
	Castle/fort
	Building of historic interest
	English Heritage
	Garden
	Nature reserve
	Water activities
	Fishing
☆	Other tourist feature

WATER FEATURES

126

Map of the British Isles

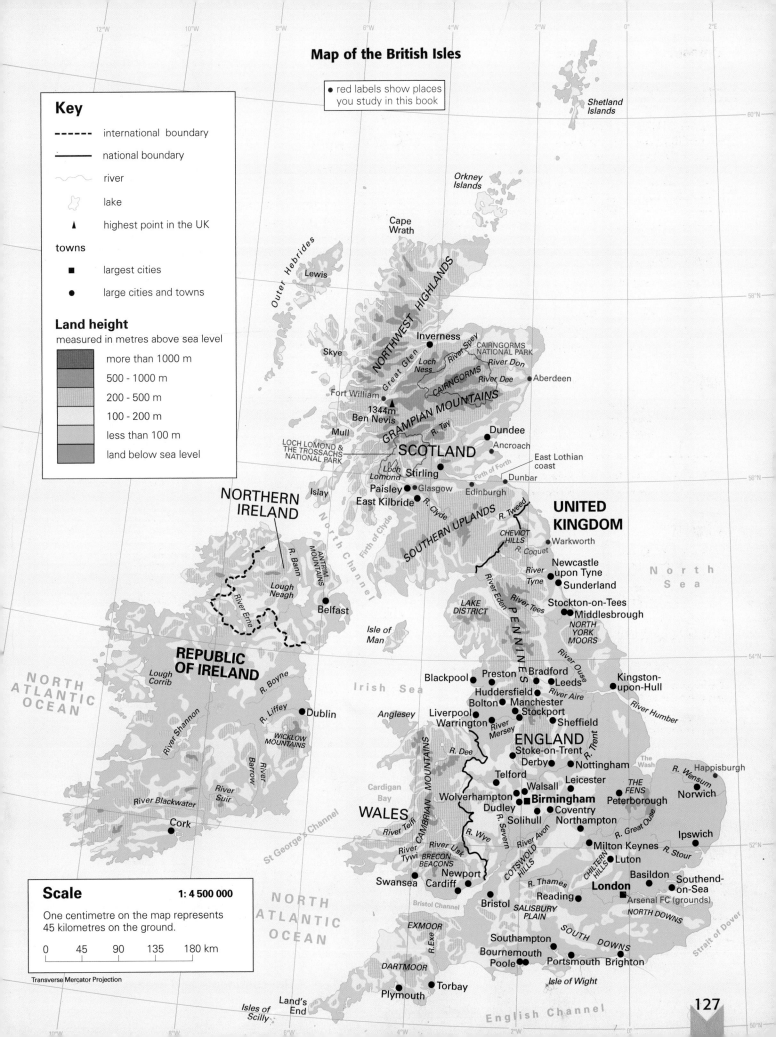

red labels show places you study in this book

Key

- – – – international boundary
- ——— national boundary
- ∿∿∿ river
- lake
- ▲ highest point in the UK

towns
- ■ largest cities
- ● large cities and towns

Land height
measured in metres above sea level

- more than 1000 m
- 500 - 1000 m
- 200 - 500 m
- 100 - 200 m
- less than 100 m
- land below sea level

Scale
1: 4 500 000

One centimetre on the map represents 45 kilometres on the ground.

0   45   90   135   180 km

Transverse Mercator Projection

Shetland Islands

Orkney Islands

Cape Wrath

Outer Hebrides

Lewis

Skye

NORTHWEST HIGHLANDS

Inverness

Loch Ness

Great Glen

River Spey

CAIRNGORMS NATIONAL PARK

River Don

River Dee

Aberdeen

Fort William

1344m Ben Nevis

CAIRNGORMS

GRAMPIAN MOUNTAINS

R. Tay

Mull

Dundee

Ancroach

SCOTLAND

LOCH LOMOND & THE TROSSACHS NATIONAL PARK

East Lothian coast

Loch Lomond

Stirling

Firth of Forth

Dunbar

Islay

Paisley

Glasgow

Edinburgh

East Kilbride

R. Clyde

UNITED KINGDOM

Firth of Clyde

R. Tweed

SOUTHERN UPLANDS

CHEVIOT HILLS

R. Coquet

Warkworth

NORTHERN IRELAND

R. Bann

ANTRIM MOUNTAINS

North Channel

River Tyne

Newcastle upon Tyne

Sunderland

River Erne

Lough Neagh

River Eden

River Tees

Stockton-on-Tees

Middlesbrough

Belfast

LAKE DISTRICT

PENNINES

NORTH YORK MOORS

North Sea

Isle of Man

River Ouse

REPUBLIC OF IRELAND

Lough Corrib

NORTH ATLANTIC OCEAN

Irish Sea

Blackpool

Preston

Bradford

Leeds

Kingston-upon-Hull

Huddersfield

River Aire

R. Boyne

Bolton

Manchester

Stockport

Anglesey

Liverpool

Sheffield

River Humber

R. Liffey

Dublin

Warrington

River Mersey

R. Shannon

WICKLOW MOUNTAINS

ENGLAND

R. Dee

Stoke-on-Trent

R. Trent

The Wash

R. Wensum

Happisburgh

Derby

Nottingham

CAMBRIAN MOUNTAINS

Telford

Leicester

Norwich

Barrow

River Suir

Cardigan Bay

Walsall

THE FENS

Wolverhampton

Birmingham

Peterborough

River Blackwater

Dudley

Coventry

Solihull

Northampton

R. Great Ouse

Ipswich

Cork

WALES

River Teifi

R. Severn

River Avon

Milton Keynes

R. Stour

St George's Channel

River Tywi

R. Wye

COTSWOLD HILLS

CHILTERN HILLS

Luton

River Usk

BRECON BEACONS

R. Thames

Basildon

London

Southend-on-Sea

Swansea

Newport

Cardiff

Reading

Arsenal FC (grounds)

NORTH ATLANTIC OCEAN

Bristol Channel

Bristol

SALISBURY PLAIN

NORTH DOWNS

EXMOOR

R. Exe

SOUTH DOWNS

Strait of Dover

Southampton

Bournemouth

Poole

Portsmouth

Brighton

DARTMOOR

Isle of Wight

Land's End

Plymouth

Torbay

Isles of Scilly

English Channel

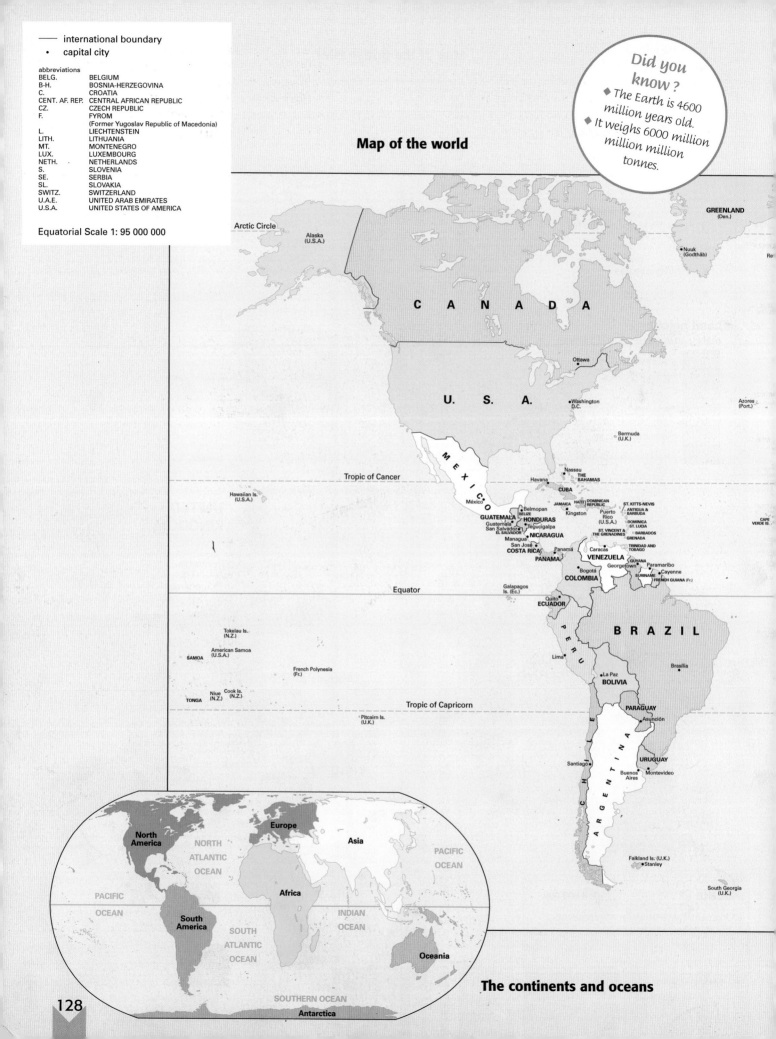

international boundary
• capital city

abbreviations
BELG.   BELGIUM
B-H.   BOSNIA-HERZEGOVINA
C.   CROATIA
CENT. AF. REP.   CENTRAL AFRICAN REPUBLIC
CZ.   CZECH REPUBLIC
F.   FYROM
  (Former Yugoslav Republic of Macedonia)
L.   LIECHTENSTEIN
LITH.   LITHUANIA
MT.   MONTENEGRO
LUX.   LUXEMBOURG
NETH.   NETHERLANDS
S.   SLOVENIA
SE.   SERBIA
SL.   SLOVAKIA
SWITZ.   SWITZERLAND
U.A.E.   UNITED ARAB EMIRATES
U.S.A.   UNITED STATES OF AMERICA

Equatorial Scale 1: 95 000 000

Map of the world

Did you know ?
◆ The Earth is 4600 million years old.
◆ It weighs 6000 million million million tonnes.

Arctic Circle

GREENLAND
(Den.)

Alaska
(U.S.A.)

Nuuk
(Godthåb)

C A N A D A

Ottawa

U. S. A.

Washington
D.C.

Azores
(Port.)

Bermuda
(U.K.)

Tropic of Cancer

Hawaiian Is.
(U.S.A.)

México

MEXICO

Havana

Nassau
THE BAHAMAS

CUBA

CAPE VERDE IS.

Belmopan
BELIZE

JAMAICA

HAITI

DOMINICAN REPUBLIC

ST. KITTS-NEVIS
ANTIGUA & BARBUDA

GUATEMALA

HONDURAS

Kingston

Puerto Rico
(U.S.A.)

DOMINICA
ST. LUCIA

Guatemala
San Salvador
EL SALVADOR

Tegucigalpa

ST. VINCENT & THE GRENADINES

BARBADOS
GRENADA

NICARAGUA

Managua

San José

COSTA RICA

Panamá

Caracas

TRINIDAD AND TOBAGO

PANAMA

VENEZUELA

GUYANA

Bogotá

Georgetown

Paramaribo

Cayenne

SURINAME

FRENCH GUIANA (Fr.)

COLOMBIA

Galapagos
Is. (Ec.)

Equator

Quito
ECUADOR

P E R U

B R A Z I L

Tokelau Is.
(N.Z.)

American Samoa
(U.S.A.)

SAMOA

French Polynesia
(Fr.)

Lima

Brasília

TONGA

Niue
(N.Z.)

Cook Is.
(N.Z.)

La Paz

BOLIVIA

Tropic of Capricorn

Pitcairn Is.
(U.K.)

PARAGUAY

Asunción

A R G E N T I N A

C H I L E

URUGUAY

Santiago

Buenos
Aires

Montevideo

Falkland Is. (U.K.)
Stanley

South Georgia
(U.K.)

North
America

Europe

Asia

NORTH
ATLANTIC
OCEAN

PACIFIC
OCEAN

PACIFIC
OCEAN

Africa

INDIAN
OCEAN

South
America

SOUTH
ATLANTIC
OCEAN

Oceania

SOUTHERN OCEAN

Antarctica

The continents and oceans

128

Amazing – but true!
◆ Nearly 70% of the Earth is covered by saltwater.
◆ Nearly 1/3 is covered by the Pacific Ocean.
◆ 10% of the land is covered by glaciers.
◆ 20% of the land is covered by deserts.

World champions
◆ Largest continent – Asia
◆ Longest river – The Nile, Egypt
◆ Highest mountain – Everest, Nepal
◆ Largest desert – Sahara, North Africa
◆ Largest ocean – Pacific

Did you know?
The world has:
◆ over 200 countries
◆ over 6 billion people
◆ over 6000 different languages.

Glossary

A

adapt – change to suit the conditions; plants have adapted to suit the climate

aerial photo – taken from the air

air mass – a huge block of air moving over the Earth; it can be warm or cold, damp or dry, depending on where it came from

air pressure – the weight of air pressing down on the Earth's surface

altitude – height of a place above sea level

anemometer – it is used to measure wind speed

aquifer – a large underground reservoir of groundwater; you can pump the water up and use it as a water supply

Arctic Circle – an imaginary line around the Earth at 66.5° north of the equator

arch – the curved outline left when the sea erodes the inside of a cave away

atmosphere – the layer of gas around the Earth

B

backwash – the water that rolls back down a beach after a wave has broken

barometer – it is used to measure air pressure

bay – a smooth curve of coast between two headlands

beach – an area made of sand or small stones deposited by waves

beach replenishment – adding sand to a beach to replace the sand that the waves have carried away

biome – a very large ecosystem

brownfield site – a site that was built on before, but can be redeveloped

C

carnivore – eats animals

CBD – central business district – the area at the centre of a town or city, with the main shops and offices

climate – the 'average' weather in a place (what it is usually like)

climate graph – a graph that shows both temperature and rainfall

cloud cover – how much of the sky is hidden by cloud; given in eighths (oktas)

coast – where the land meets the sea

coastal defences – barriers built to protect the coast from erosion; for example groynes and sea walls

condense – to change from gas to liquid

contour line – line on a map joining places that are the same height above sea level

conurbation – a large built-up area formed when towns and cities spread and join

convection current – a current of warmer material; when air gets warmed up, it rises in convection currents

convectional rainfall – caused by the land warming the air; the warm air rises and cools, so its water vapour condenses

converge – head towards each other; meet

D

deciduous forest – in this ecosystem, the trees lose their leaves in winter

decline – die away

delta – flat area of deposited material at the mouth of a river, where it enters the sea

densely populated – lots of people live there

deposit – to drop material; waves deposit sand and small stones in sheltered parts of the coast, forming beaches

depression – a weather system made up of two fronts, a warm front chased by a cold one; it brings wet windy weather

derelict – run-down and abandoned

desalinate – remove the salt (from sea water)

desert – an area with less than 250 mm of rain a year; it can be hot, cool, or cold

developed country – has a good standard of living (good schools, roads and so on)

developers – companies that buy land and put up buildings for rent or sale

dwelling – a building to live in

E

economic – about money, business, and earning a living

economic activity – work you get paid for

ecosystem – a unit made up of living things and their non-living environment; for example a pond, a forest, a desert

embankment – a bank of earth or concrete built up on a river bank, to prevent floods

environment – everything around you; the air, soil, rivers and climate are part of our natural environment

equator – an imaginary line around the middle of the Earth (at 0° latitude)

erosion – the wearing away of rock, stones and soil by rivers, waves, wind or glaciers

evaporation – the change from liquid to gas

eye (of a hurricane) – the calm clear area in the centre of a hurricane, with no cloud

eye wall – the thick cloud around the eye of a hurricane

F

fetch – the length of water the wind blows over, before it meets the coast

flood – an overflow of water from a river

fossil fuels – coal, oil, and natural gas; they are the remains of plants and animals that lived millions of years ago

front – the leading edge of an air mass; a warm front means a warm air mass is arriving

frontal rainfall – rain caused by a warm front meeting a cold one

G

geology – the study of rocks

glacier – a river of ice

global warming – the way temperatures around the world are rising

greenfield site – it has not been built on before

greenhouse gases – gases like carbon dioxide and methane that trap heat around the Earth, giving global warming

groundwater – rainwater that has soaked down through the ground and filled up the cracks in the rock below

groynes – barriers of wood or stone down a beach, to stop sand being washed away

H

headland – land that juts out into the sea

herbivore – an animal that eats only plants

hurricane – a violent spinning storm system bringing high winds, rain, and storm surges

hydraulic action – the action of water pressure in breaking up rock

I

indigenous people – the very first settlers in a country, and their descendents

Industrial Revolution – the time around the 18th century when many new machines were invented and many factories built

industry – a branch of manufacturing or trade; for example the car industry

infrastructure – the basic services in a place, such as roads, railways, water supply

international – to do with more than one country

irrigate – to pipe water to crops, where there is not enough rain

isotherm – line on a map joining places with the same temperature

L

landform – a feature formed by erosion or deposition (such as a spit, bay, beach)

latitude – how far a place is north or south of the equator, in degrees

levee – a bank or embankment built along a river, to prevent flooding

leeward – sheltered from the wind

local – to do with the area around you

longitude – how far a place is east or west of the prime meridian, in degrees

longshore drift – how sand and other material is carried parallel to the shore, by the waves

long-term – for many years ahead

M

merchandise – goods for sale

meteorologist – studies weather and climate

monsoon season – the season in south Asia when warm moist winds blow in from the sea, bringing lots of rain

N

national – to do with the whole country (for example the national anthem)

National Park – a large area of land protected by law for everyone to enjoy

nocturnal – comes out at night

nomads – people who do not settle in one place, but move from place to place

North Atlantic Drift – a warm current in the Atlantic Ocean; it keeps the weather on the west coast of Britain mild in winter

O

oasis – a place in the desert where groundwater is close to the surface; so plants grow well, and people can farm

OS map – a detailed map, that uses a special set of symbols, produced by a body called the Ordnance Survey

P

pastoralists – people who rear plant-eating animals for a living; they move with them to find pasture (grass to eat)

permafrost – the soil in the tundra that is permanently frozen

photosynthesis – how plants make their food from carbon dioxide and water

plan – a map of a small area (such as the school, or a room) drawn to scale

pollution – anything that spoils the environment; for example traffic fumes, factory waste, oil spills, litter, noise

population – the number of people living in a place

population density – the average number of people per square kilometre; to find it, divide population by area (in sq km)

precipitation – water falling from the sky (as rain, sleet, hail, snow)

prevailing wind – the wind that blows most often; in the UK it is a south west wind (it blows *from* the south west)

primary sector – the part of the economy where people take things from the Earth and sea (farming, fishing, mining)

prime meridian – the imaginary line from which longitude is measured; it passes through Greenwich in London

public enquiry – where people can give their point of view, for example about plans for a new road

Q

quaternary sector – the part of the economy where people do high-tech research (for example into genes)

R

rain shadow – area sheltered from the rain by a hill or mountain

redevelop – to rebuild an area for a new use

relief rainfall – rain caused by the wind being forced to rise over a hill or mountain

residential area – an area that is mainly homes (rather than shops or offices)

rock armour – rocks piled up to protect the coast from erosion

rural area – an area of countryside, where people live on farms and in villages

S

salt marsh – a low-lying marshy area by the sea, with salty water from the tides

satellite image – a picture taken by a camera carried on a satellite

scale – the ratio of the distance on a map to the real distance

secondary sector – the part of the economy where people make or manufacture things (such as cars or furniture)

sediment – a layer of material (stones, sand and mud) deposited by a river

settlement – a place where people live; it could be a hamlet, village, town or city

settler – a person who takes over land to live on, where no one has lived before

shingle – small pebbles

short-term – just for the days and weeks ahead

silt – fine particles of soil carried by rivers

site – the land a settlement is built on

situation – where a settlement is, relative to things like rivers, hills, other settlements

social – about people and the way they live

sparsely populated – few people live there

spit – a strip of sand or shingle in the sea

spot height – the exact height at a spot on an OS map (look for a dot and a number)

stack – a pillar of rock left standing in the sea when the top of an arch collapses

storm surge – a huge wave of water drawn up and carried onto land by a hurricane

stump – the remains of a stack which the sea has eroded away

succulents – plants that can store up water

sustainable – brings economic, social and environmental benefits, and can be carried on without future harm

swash – the water that rushes up the beach when a wave breaks

T

temperature – how hot or cold something is, measured in degrees Centigrade

tertiary sector – the part of the economy where people provide services (for example teachers, doctors, taxi drivers)

thermometer – it is used to measure temperature

tides – the rise and fall in sea level, due mainly to the pull of the moon

transport – the carrying away of material by rivers, waves, the wind or glaciers

tropical rainforests – the thick forests that grow in the tropics, where it rains a lot

tropical storm – a storm system with fierce winds, that may develop into a hurricane

tropics – the area between the Tropic of Cancer and the Tropic of Capricorn

tundra – an ecosystem with a very cold dry climate, that lies around the North Pole

U

urban area – a built-up area, such as a town or city; it's the opposite of rural

urban regeneration – when a run-down urban area is redeveloped and brought to life again

U-shaped valley – a valley shaped like the letter U, carved out by a glacier

V

valley – an area with higher land on each side; it often has a river flowing in it

vegetation – trees, grass, and other plants

visibility – how far you can see; on a foggy day it could be just 1 or 2 metres

V-shaped valley – a valley shaped like the letter V, carved out by a river

W

water cycle – water is evaporated from the sea, falls as rain, and returns to the sea in rivers

water vapour – water in gas form

weather – the state of the atmosphere; for example how warm, wet or windy it is

weathering – the breaking down of rock; it is caused mainly by the weather

windward – facing into the wind

wave-cut notch – a notch in a cliff face, cut by the waves

wave-cut platform – the flat rocky area left behind when waves erode a cliff away

wind – air in motion

wind direction – where the wind blows *from*

wind speed – how fast the wind blows

wind vane – it shows the wind's direction

Index